THE STRUCTURE OF OBSCURITY

THE STRUCTURE OF OBSCURITY: GERTRUDE STEIN, LANGUAGE, AND CUBISM

RANDA DUBNICK

UNIVERSITY OF ILLINOIS PRESS
URBANA AND CHICAGO

This book is printed on acid-free paper.

Frontispiece: 1. Pablo Picasso, *Gertrude Stein,* 1906. 39⅜ × 32″.
THE METROPOLITAN MUSEUM OF ART, BEQUEST OF GERTRUDE STEIN, 1946.

LIBRARY OF CONGRESS CATALOGING IN PUBLICATION DATA

Dubnick, Randa K.
   The structure of obscurity.

   Bibliography: p.
   Includes index.
   1. Stein, Gertrude, 1874–1946—Style.   2. Cubism and
literature.   3. Stein, Gertrude, 1874–1946—Knowledge—
Art.   4. Structuralism (Literary analysis)   5. Aphasia.
I. Title.
PS3537.T323Z588   1983   818′.5209   83–3603
ISBN 0–252–00909–6

FOR MEL,
FOR HEATHER AND PHILIP,
AND FOR MY PARENTS

CONTENTS

ILLUSTRATIONS

ACKNOWLEDGMENTS

W HATEVER IS VALUABLE in these pages has been in some measure influenced by the persons whose names appear below; whatever flaws there may be are my own.

Above all I owe a debt of gratitude to Kaye Howe of the University of Colorado. She was generous with advice and encouragement as a few ideas about cubism, structuralism, and Gertrude Stein developed into a dissertation, which she directed. Others at the University of Colorado who influenced the approach and shape of this book include Ed Nolan, Sophia Morgan, Ulrich Goldsmith, Ed Rivers, Esther Zago, and Mary Berg.

I am indebted to Timothy Mitchell of the department of art history at the University of Kansas for reading and reacting to chapters 1 and 2, and for many valuable insights about cubism. Dale Dillinger of the University of Kansas and Herman Rappaport of Loyola University of Chicago generously contributed suggestions about structuralism and linguistics. I am also indebted, for valuable comments and reactions, to the persons who reviewed my manuscript for the University of Illinois Press, and to Frank O. Williams of the Press for his patient and persistent support of this project and for his practical advice.

I am grateful to the University of Kansas for supplying me with a small research grant that helped to prepare the final manuscript and secure the illustrations. June Ward typed the final manuscript with great speed and the last minute revisions with patience. Ronald Walker of Loyola University of Chicago, along with Merle Lufen and her staff, generously provided a typist for an early draft of the manuscript.

For assistance in locating some of the works used herein as illustrations, I am indebted to the department of rights and reproductions, the department of twentieth-century painting, and the librarians at the Art Institute of Chicago, as well as the department of rights and reproductions at the Museum of Modern Art in New York. I am grateful also to the institutions and individuals who kindly allowed me to use works from their collections to illustrate this book.

My husband Mel has been an enormous help: without his encouragement, wit, and great assistance with practical matters this book could not have been completed. He now knows more about Gertrude Stein than any other political scientist in the country. I would also like to thank my children for riddles, giggles, and other pleasant interruptions.

G ERTRUDE STEIN'S WRITING has presented difficulties to many readers, and traditional literary criticism has not been able to help very much. Michael Hoffman points out that "Gertrude Stein's writings do not fit into the mainstream of twentieth century criticism," partly because most critics, influenced by "analytic psychology, both Freudian and Jungian, and cultural anthropology" are

> inclined to look at literature primarily in terms of its symbolism, both analytic and archetypal, and its use of myth and ritual. . . . But the student of Gertrude Stein is offered slim rewards in this direction. . . . If in Joyce's writing subject matter is so enriched that any allusion may have innumerable possible referents, then in Gertrude Stein the subject matter is reduced to almost non-existence and seemingly nothing is left but pure sound and syntax. It is ostensibly a task for the philologist, and the student of literature has continually thrown up his hands at what he does not understand.[1]

The twentieth-century audience has often had to struggle to catch up with its artists, but an audience has been created for many artistic innovators, such as Picasso, Joyce, Eliot, and Woolf. Stein's audience

has been slow to catch up with her, partly because of this lack of referential material for traditional literary criticism and readers.

Because of Stein's innovative use of language—she uses words as if
they were new and had no history—she has often been dismissed as
merely eccentric or simpleminded. Yet the aesthetic sensibility and
foresight of this woman have been demonstrated by art history. The
enduring fortunes of Picasso and his influence on modern art have made
apparent the accuracy of Stein's judgment about him. As W. G. Rogers
put it, "Those who scorn Stein the writer are obliged by historical fact
to accept Stein the collector, for the pictures picked almost fifty years
ago by her alone, or sometimes with Leo, today fill the art magazines,
draw the largest crowds to galleries and museums, and fetch the highest
prices."[2] Now, three-quarters of the way through the twentieth century,
Dada, surrealism, the theater of the absurd, and minimal and conceptual art have all become accepted and even familiar. Still, it has been a
long wait for a critical approach that can prepare the reader for Gertrude
Stein's writing. However, the development of structuralism as a critical
method of the late fifties and sixties has led to a relatively new way into
her work.[3] Because Stein's writing does emphasize sound and syntax,
insights from linguistics and semiology are useful tools in Stein criticism.

An analysis of Stein's obscurity made in light of some insights about
language from structuralism reveals two kinds of linguistically consistent obscure styles in her oeuvre. Stein called the first style *prose* and
the second style *poetry*. Her definition of each genre and her description of these two obscure styles suggest some of the dualistic distinctions about language that have been made by structuralists and
semiologists, such as Saussure, Barthes, and Jakobson, as will be seen
in the following chapters. Each of Stein's obscure styles emphasizes
one of the two basic linguistic operations identified by structuralist Roman
Jakobson as *selection* (choice of signifying elements: vocabulary) and
combination (ordering of elements: spatial or syntactic).

In addition, the works of structuralists Jakobson and Barthes, both
of whom expand Saussure's linguistic theories to realms beyond verbal
language, are useful in dealing with Stein since their ideas provide a
nonmetaphorical way of dealing with frequently drawn analogies between cubism and Stein's writing.[4]

Stein was linked with the cubist movement not only by her friendship
with Picasso, but also by her conviction that her work resembled his in
many ways. She said of Picasso, "I was alone at this time in understanding him, perhaps because I was expressing the same thing in lit-

erature."[5] When one compares Stein's writing with cubist painting in light of structuralist theories, it becomes clear that like Stein's writing, cubism in its two major phases—analytic and synthetic—manifests two different types of obscurity, each emphasizing one of those same two linguistic operations identified by Jakobson. Even though words and pictures are quite different entities, the operations of selection and combination are used similarly in the parallel styles of Stein's writing and cubist painting. The similarity between Stein's writing and cubist painting seems based on common emphases on certain operations of signification over others.[6] So structuralist theories indicate that Stein's attempts to emulate cubism *are* appropriate to literature because they concern the very nature of language.

Much misunderstanding of Stein's work is based either on underreading—seeing too little meaning in her work and regarding it as empty words—or on overreading—insisting on finding discursive meaning where none exists. Both erroneous approaches reflect a rejection of obscurity. But as D. C. Yalden-Thompson said, "It is precisely Gertrude Stein's obscurity which is the challenge to anyone who takes her seriously."[7]

At one extreme are those who believe that Stein makes no sense; at the other are those who go too far in explicating her. Too often the underlying assumption is that her writing is nonsense (a view held by amiable and antagonistic critics alike): that her work is all sound, perhaps even random sound, without sense. Of course, Stein's writing always does contain meaning, at the very least in the sense that every signifier calls up a signified, a mental construct. Stein herself maintained that it is impossible to make no sense at all:

> I took individual words and thought about them until I got their weight and volume complete and put them next to another word, and at this same time I found out very soon that there is no such thing as putting them together without sense. . . . I made innumerable efforts to make words write without sense and found it impossible. Any human being putting down words had to make sense of them.[8]

At the other extreme are those who go so far in trying to show that Stein's writing contains (hidden) meaning—e.g., discursive or sexual — that they overexplicate her work.

One can certainly find discursive meaning in most of Stein's public writing (e.g., autobiographies and lectures) and even in certain lines of her most apparently nonsensical works. But some critics search so zealously for meaning that they find it even in the most obscure and non-discursive lines. This kind of overreading is based on the same underlying assumption as the dismissal of her work as *non-sense*: that only discursive meaning justifies the existence of literature. If Stein's work is to be rejected, it will be because it lacks discursive meaning. If it is to be saved, critics must show that discursive meaning lies hidden in every (or nearly every) line of her work.

But this is impossible. Some of Stein's writing contains such meaning, much of it easily accessible. But some of her works and some individual lines in almost all of her works are, as Edmund Wilson puts it, "absolutely unintelligible even to a sympathetic reader."[9] Although any particular Stein piece contains some lines or passages that are meaningful in the traditional expository sense, those passages are often juxtaposed with a good deal of wordplay and apparently arbitrary language. Stein often produced readily intelligible sentences, such as the following from *The Making of Americans*: "Under Julia's very American face, body, clothes and manner and her vigor of the domineering and crude virgin, there were now and then flashes of passion that lit up an older well hidden tradition."[10] In this same book, there are many sentences that communicate much less information, due to the minimal semantic content of the vague and indefinite vocabulary: "When he was one being one at the ending of beginning being living he was almost needing being one going to be doing some other thing sometime" (p. 876). Often Stein produced unintelligible sentences that were grammatically sound but combined words without regard for whether the mental constructs evoked by them mirrored referential reality, as in the following sentences from *Tender Buttons*: "Water is squeezing, water is almost squeezing on lard."[11] And some of Stein's "sentences" are unintelligible partly because they are not sentences at all, as in the following passage from *Tender Buttons*: "Alas, alas the pull alas the bell alas the coach in china, alas the little put in leaf alas the wedding butter meat, alas the receptacle, alas the back shape of mussle, mussle and soda" (p. 53). Evident here is a variety in Stein's writing that renders inadequate flat statements that she is obscure.

In the first place, not all of Stein's work is unintelligible. And within that part of her work which is obscure, there are two distinct styles that might be called abstract, each representing a linguistically different kind of obscurity: the first evident in *The Making of Americans* and literary "portraits" written circa 1909–11, the second in *Tender Buttons* and other works written around 1912 or shortly afterward. Her writing beyond this point develops and combines these two types of obscurity.

Using insights about language contributed by structuralists like Barthes and Jakobson, it becomes possible to arrive at a stylistic analysis of the two distinct ways in which Stein's writing moves toward the abstract and becomes obscure. This leads to an understanding that Stein moves toward *abstractionism* in two different ways and to a clearer notion of how that term should be used in describing her writing, especially in comparing her writing with cubism.

Once it is understood what Stein's two major obscure styles (prose and poetry) are like and how their development parallels that of analytic and synthetic cubism, it will be easier to understand the further stylistic changes that took place in her writing when cubism ceased to be a major influence: the disintegration of sentences into lists or columns of words that appeared in her poetry and drama in the twenties, and the reemergence of syntax in the relatively clear prose of the thirties.

Since Stein's writing is largely made up of variations and combinations of the two stylistic and linguistic preoccupations represented by the participial style of *The Making of Americans* and the noun-centered style of *Tender Buttons*, one must begin by examining those two works to understand her stylistic development.

THE STRUCTURE OF OBSCURITY

Rㅏ ICHARD BRIDGMAN AND EDMUND WILSON are among those who attribute the relative unintelligibility of Stein's work to her need to write about private passions while also needing to be discreet about their nature. As Stein might have said herself, "Interesting, if true." But the only real relevance of this sexually motivated evasiveness to Stein's style is as a possible impetus for her linguistic innovations. In *The Making of Americans* (and other stylistically similar works), Stein stretches the contiguity of the sentence as far as it will go without snapping, while simultaneously reducing to a minimum the vocabulary available for selection. In *Tender Buttons* and similar works, the available vocabulary becomes practically limitless, while the syntax is shortened, destroyed, and even disintegrates into lists. Roman Jakobson's observations about language indicate that conventional intelligibility only occurs when both aspects of language are fully operative.[1] To say that Stein's innovations grew out of some sort of personal desire or need to be unintelligible may be speculative. But one *can* say with more certainty that her obscurity was a necessary consequence of her innovative approach as she created two different types of obscurity.

John Golding writes that by 1909 "Picasso and Braque had initiated the first phase of cubism."[2] In this first stage

The whole picture surface is brought to life by the interaction of the shaded, angular planes. Some of these planes seem to recede away from the eye into shallow depth, but this sensation is always counteracted by a succeeding passage which will lead the eye forward again up on to the picture plane. The optical sensation produced is comparable to that of running one's hand over an immensely elaborate, subtly carved sculpture in low relief.[3]

As forms became increasingly difficult to read, color was limited to browns, ochres, and grays, as in Picasso's *Portrait of D.H. Kahnweiler* (Autumn 1910) (Plate 2) and *Portrait of Wilhelm Uhde* (1910) (Plate 3). In these portraits, it is evident that the paintings are still representational, however difficult they are to "read." This stage of cubism is usually referred to as *analytic cubism*, as distinct from *synthetic cubism*, the second main stage, which followed around 1912.[4]

During the phase of analytic cubism (1909 to 1911–12), marked by monochromatic gray paintings that broke the subject matter down into repetitive, overlapping planes, Stein was finishing *The Making of Americans* (1909–11)[5] and writing portraits such as "Picasso" and "Matisse"[6] characterized by repeated clauses, extended syntax, and a vague, constricted vocabulary. Although obscure, this style is still mimetic, as is analytic cubism.

Stein called this first style, which was concerned with sentences, *prose*. Both Picasso and Stein, in their pre-1912 work, present the fleeting, fragmentary nature of perception, and represent the integrity of the individual moment of perception before consolidation by memory into a conceptual whole. In Stein's first type of obscurity and in Picasso's analytic phase, constriction of vocabulary, verbal or pictorial, increases obscurity. In both a barely perceptible presence lies behind a translucent surface of lines or words.

The first stage of cubism eventually evolved into the second stage—synthetic cubism—usually marked around 1912, with the introduction of collage.[7] Picasso's *Still Life with Chair Caning* (early 1912) is said to be the first collage.[8] (See Plate 4). In this second phase the cubists began to use pictorial elements plastically, often composing works in which "the original compositional ideas may have been developed by the arrangement of a few abstract pictorial shapes" that suggested a subject[9] rather than beginning with a subject that is analyzed. Compared with the first stage, pictorial elements in the second stage, such as color and texture, are used with much greater variety and richness,[10] as in Picasso's *Guitar and Wine Glass* (1912) (Plate 5) and his *Green Still Life* (1914) (Plate 6). Around 1912 a marked change also developed in Gertrude Stein's style. This change is evident in works like *Two: Gertrude Stein and Her Brother* and *G.M.P.* (also known as *Matisse, Picasso, and Gertrude Stein*) (both 1911–12), in which style changes radically in mid-book; but it is epitomized by *Tender Buttons* (1912).[11] This style is centered on the word rather than the sentence, as vocabulary is extended and syntax degenerates into sentence fragments. In these works, representation—the prosaic use of words to represent verbal experience through description—is subordinated to the use of words as words, with emphasis on their "plastic" or poetic qualities.

At this time, apparently both Stein and the cubists fully realized that signifying elements could be used much more arbitrarily than in the past to produce an independent object that was no longer basically mimetic.[12] For both Stein and Picasso, with this realization came the production of more still lifes, more attention to signifying elements for their own sake, and a playful lyricism. In Stein's second style and in synthetic cubism, the vocabulary of signifying elements (words for Stein, color and texture for Picasso) is extended, while the relationship between signifying element and subject matter becomes arbitrary. While vocabulary is extended in Stein's second obscure style and synthetic cubism, syntax—grammatical or spatial—is suppressed by the disintegration of the sentence and its traditional organization, and by a use of the picture plane that emphasizes its flat surface more than its traditional illusion of depth. Both Stein's second obscure style and synthetic cubism play games with traditional syntax (grammatical or spatial) rather than use it straight forwardly. Both force attention to the art object as a thing in itself, an opaque object to be looked *at* rather than *through*.

Stein saw this stylistic shift as a change from prose, with its concern for the sentence (syntax), to poetry, with its concern for the noun (vocabulary). In the famous lecture "Poetry and Grammar," written in 1934,[13] Gertrude Stein explains the radical stylistic difference between *The Making of Americans* and *Tender Buttons* as the difference between prose and poetry. Prose is made of sentences and paragraphs, whereas poetry focuses on vocabulary, particularly the noun.

> In The Making of Americans . . . a very long prose book made up of sentences and paragraphs . . . I had gotten rid of nouns and adjectives as much as possible by the method of living in adverbs in verbs in pronouns in adverbial clauses written or implied and in conjunctions.[14]

> . . . really great written prose is bound to be made up more of verbs adverbs prepositions prepositional clauses and conjunctions

than nouns. The vocabulary in prose of course is important if you
like vocabulary is always important. . . .[15]

However, she states that "the vocabulary in respect to prose is less
important than the parts of speech, and the internal balance and the
movement within a given space." On the other hand, "Poetry has to do
with vocabulary just as prose has not. . . . Poetry is I say essentially a
vocabulary just as prose is essentially not. . . . And what is the vocabulary of which poetry absolutely is. It is a vocabulary entirely based on
the noun as prose is essentially and determinately and vigorously not
based on the noun."[16]

In distinguishing this emphasis on syntax in prose from poetry's emphasis on diction, Stein touches upon what structural linguists call the
horizontal and *vertical axes of language* (as formulated by Saussure,
Jakobson, and Barthes, with somewhat varying terminology). The horizontal axis links words contiguously. Roland Barthes defines it as:

> [A] combination of signs, which has space as a support. In the
> articulated language, this space is linear and irreversible (it is the
> "spoken chain"): two elements cannot be pronounced at the same
> time (*re-enter, against all, human life*): each term here derives its
> value from its opposition to what precedes and what follows; in
> the chain of speech, the terms are really united *in praesentia*.[17]

When Stein says that the key element in prose is the sentence, and that
verbs, prepositions, and conjunctions (which function to hold the syntax of the sentence together) are important in prose, she implies emphasis on the horizontal axis of language. On the other hand, Barthes points
out that the vertical axis of language links words by associations based
on similarity and/or opposition, and has to do with the selection of
words.

> "Beside the discourse (syntagmatic plane), the units which have
> something in common are associated in memory and thus form
> groups within which various relationships can be found": *educa-
> tion* can be associated, through its meaning, to *upbringing* or
> *training*, and through its sound, to *educate, educator*, or to *appli-
> cation, vindication*. . . . [I]n each series, unlike what happens at
> the syntagmatic level, the terms are united *in absentia*.[18]

Stein says poetry's key concern is vocabulary, the noun in particular.
In poetry then, word choice (vocabulary) is more important than syn-
tax, which may even be suppressed, especially in modern poetry. In
Writing Degree Zero, Roland Barthes says:

[M]odern poetry . . . destroys the spontaneously functional nature of language, and leaves standing only its lexical basis. . . . The Word shines forth above a line of relationships emptied of their content, grammar is bereft of its purpose, it becomes prosody and is no longer anything but an inflexion which lasts only to present the Word.[19]

Furthermore, Barthes says, in poetry, "The Word . . . is encyclopaedic, it contains simultaneously all the acceptations from which a relational discourse might have required it to choose. It therefore achieves a state which is possible only in the dictionary or in poetry."[20]

Choosing a word from a group of synonyms on the criteria of rhythm and rhyme or choosing a poetic vocabulary from within an entire language is an operation of selection. According to structural linguistic theories, the operation of selection functions along the vertical axis of language. On this basis Roman Jakobson has also distinguished between poetry and prose: "The principle of similarity underlies poetry; the metrical parallelism of lines or the phonic equivalence of rhyming words prompts the question of semantic similarity and contrast. . . . Prose, on the contrary, is forwarded essentially by contiguity."[21]

As to Stein's remarks about the various parts of speech, Ronald Levinson notes that Stein's theoretical formulation of the functions of the parts of speech was apparently greatly influenced by the theories of William James.[22] William James, in *Psychology*, compared the "stream of consciousness" to a series of "flights and perchings"; the perchings being substantives ("occupied by sensorial imaginings") and the flights being transitives ("thoughts of relating, static and dynamic") that depend on verbs, prepositions, and conjunctions.[23] As Levinson points out, the philosophy of grammar set forth in Stein's "Poetry and Grammar" echoes some of James's theories,[24] especially the distinction between static words (nouns) and dynamic words (verbs, prepositions).

Miss Stein is urging a program of linguistic usage which, though definitely outrunning James' demands . . . is nevertheless founded upon a conception of the "stream of consciousness" quite similar to that of James. Her accent on the more fluid and moving elements in language (the verbs and adverbs), her corresponding depreciation of the static moveless noun, what is this but the counterpart of James' plea in behalf of the "flights" as against the linguistic predominance of the "perchings"? And perhaps the most striking, though by no means the most fundamental, point of parallelism between them is the prominence they both accord to conjunctions and prepositions, the often unappreciated parts of speech.[25]

What is original is Stein's use of James's theories as the basis for distinguishing between poetry and prose. Prose is based on verbs, prepositions, and conjunctions (the flights): the words that support syntax. These words function along the horizontal axis and have to do with contiguity: they *combine* to hold the words of the sentence in relation to one another. Poetry, on the other hand, is based on the noun or the substantive (the perchings). Roman Jakobson's linguistic analysis of two types of obscurity produced by the suppression of each of the two basic linguistic operations indicates that the noun is closely associated with the operation of selection (the vertical axis).[26] So Stein's distinction between prose and poetry is based not merely on stylistic or formal considerations but, rather, on two linguistic, and even mental, operations that structuralists have since identified as *similarity* (or selection or system) and *contiguity* (or combination or syntagm).

Though one can see the germs of some of these ideas in William James's theories as set forth in *Psychology*, Stein extends the ideas and applies them in her creative writing. James describes consciousness as a continuous flow, distinguishes between static and dynamic parts of speech, and discerns several types of association. One of these is based on contiguity, meaning habitual association of things previously experienced as existing together in time and space.[27] James also discusses "association by similarity," based on similarity of entities that are not linked in space or time.[28] "Now two compound things are similar when some one quality or qualities is shared alike by both, although as regards their other qualities they have nothing in common. The moon resembles a gas jet, it also is similar to a football; but a gas jet and a football are not similar to each other."[29] However, James neither extends this distinction from the realm of association nor uses it to split all linguistic operations along these lines as do theories of structuralism.

Stein has contributed to the creation of an aesthetic based on James's theories and on pragmatism in general, as Robert Haas points out:

> It is little surprising that the ideas of William James have influenced his pupil. . . . It is to be understood literally that the rudiments of a pragmatic aesthetic appeared in her work before contemporary philosophers, including William James, had expounded such an aesthetic. . . .
>
> The whole of her creative writing seems to be the natural expression of this aesthetics in works of art. . . .
>
> If William James, as Ralph Barton Perry would have it, "was left to develop an indigenous American philosophy, the first, per-

haps, in which the American experience escaped the stamp of an imported ideology," students of Gertrude Stein would assert that it was left to her to go beyond James and to develop an indigenous American aesthetic.[30]

Through this effort she arrives at two types of obscurity that function, perhaps coincidentally, as practical illustrations of linguistic theories which were not yet published. Even the first and most limited formulation of these structural theories, in Ferdinand de Saussure's *Course in General Linguistics*, was not published until 1915, approximately three years after *Tender Buttons* was written around 1912. Furthermore, Stein's writing, which suppresses first the vertical axis at the expense of the horizontal axis and then vice versa, foreshadows Jakobson's observations about the results of sublimation of first one, and then another, of the two basic linguistic operations. Jakobson observed the sublimation of these linguistic operations in aphasic speech; he did not publish these observations until 1956.[31]

The key stylistic interest in *The Making of Americans* and in other works of Stein's participial style is syntax. Grammatically correct but eccentric sentences spin themselves out and grow, clause linked to clause, to paragraph length. Stein asserts, nothing "has ever been more exciting than diagramming sentences. . . . I like the feeling the everlasting feeling of sentences as they diagram themselves."[32] Stein's long, repetitive sentences convey a sense of process and duration, and of the time it takes to know a person or understand an idea. Stein said: "Sentences are not emotional but paragraphs are. . . . I found this out first in listening to Basket my dog drinking. And anybody listening to any dog's drinking will see what I mean."[33] The syntax or "internal" balance of the sentence is given, but the paragraph is emotional because it prolongs the duration of the idea or perception until the writer feels satisfied. This feeling of satisfaction is the similarity between a dog's drinking and the paragraph. It is a subjective feeling of having had enough that is not arrived at by following the grammatical rules. By stretching the sentence to approximately the length of a short paragraph, Stein tried to create an emotional sentence.

Many of the stylistic idiosyncracies of Stein's participial style function to extend sentence length, as in this passage located near the end of *The Making of Americans* (p. 801):

Certainly he was one being living when he was being a young one, he was often then quite certainly one being almost completely interested in being one being living, he was then quite often wanting to be one being completely interested in being one being liv-

ing. He certainly then went on being living, he did this thing certainly
all of his being living in being in young living. He certainly when
he was a young one was needing then sometimes to be sure that
he was one being living, this is certainly what some being living
are needing when they are ones being young ones in being living.
David Hersland certainly was one almost completely one being
living when he was being a young one. Some he was knowing
then were not quite completely being ones being living then, some
were quite a good deal not being ones being completely living then
when they were being young ones in being living. David Hersland
did a good deal of living in being living then when he was a young
one. He was knowing very many then and very many knew him
then. He remembered some of them in his later living and he did
not remember some of them. He certainly was one almost completely then interested in being one being living then.

In this typical paragraph, made up of only nine sentences, Stein uses
many grammatical and stylistic strategies to extend the syntax and
physical duration of the utterance.

She creates here very complex sentences, such as "Some he was
knowing then were not quite completely being ones being living then,
some were quite a good deal not being ones being completely living
then when they were being young ones in being living." But although
Stein links clause to clause, she often suppresses relative pronouns such
as *that* or *who*. In her lecture "The Gradual Making of *The Making of
Americans*," she says, "And my sentences grew longer and longer, my
imaginary dependent clauses were constantly being dropped out."[34] This
makes it harder to divide the sentences into individual clauses, and thus
forces readers into a more active role as they struggle to follow the
sentence structure.

Another simple but less orthodox way in which Stein extends syntax
is by fusing two or more sentences with commas: "He certainly then
went on being living, he did this thing certainly all of his being living
in being in young living." Her infamously infrequent use of commas
also makes readers more active (just as cubism demands a more active
role of the viewer). In "Poetry and Grammar," she says of the comma:
"And what does a comma do, a comma does nothing but make easy a
thing that if you like it enough is easy enough without the comma. A
long complicated sentence should force itself upon you, make you know
yourself knowing it."[35]

Another device for stretching the sentence to near paragraph length
is the mechanistic linking of many independent clauses together with a
series of conjunctions:

> Some are certainly needing to be ones doing something and they are doing one thing and doing it again and again and again and again and they are doing another thing and they are doing it again and again and again and they are doing another thing and they are doing it again and again and again and such a one might have been one doing a very different thing then and doing another very different thing then and doing another very different thing then and doing that then each or any one of them and doing it again and again and again. (*The Making of Americans*, p. 804.)

This first obscure style is full of participles used as nouns, adjectives, and even verb forms. Hoffman discusses the philosophical implications of this use of the present participle to prolong the time span to achieve a sense of duration and process. He points out that the present participle enhances the sense of process and the perception of an action as a continuously occurring process or continuous present.[36] The participle and the gerund also help portray the pragmatic conception of the world as a constant event. The phrase *he was one being living* (*The Making of Americans*, p. 801) conveys the process of life more fully than the relatively static phrase *he was alive*. In the first phrase, no end point is placed on the action, whereas in the second the action must be presumed to have ended at the time the phrase was written.

Stein presented each moment of perception in isolation because of her belief that all authentic perception exists in the present tense. Remembering is inauthentic and confusing, whereas knowing is a phenomenon of the present. Stein emphasized the present tense by prolonging it. Through almost exclusive reliance on the present participle ("being alive") she tried to create a continuous present, the illusion of an indefinitely extended present.

It is also important that when Stein substitutes "When he was being a young one" for "When he was young," the sentence is lengthened by four syllables. As Hoffman says, "the present participle has the partial effect of slowing down or distorting the ordinary syntactical rhythm we usually associate with standard English."[37] This substitution of the participle for a simpler form of the verb has the cumulative effect of substantially lengthening the Stein sentence, especially since, according to Hoffman, "[P]robably more than half her verb forms use some form of the progressive ending."[38] The Stein sentence is also lengthened because, as Hoffman points out, she so often insists on the "changing of an adjective into a substantive. Rather than saying 'Everybody is real,' Miss Stein changes 'real' into 'a real one.' "[39] In Chomskian terms, Stein is interested in expanding a kernel sentence into a longer, more complex, and often more ambiguous syntactic structure. For example, *being* in the phrase *one being living* can be read as either a noun or a verb, so that the phrase can be read as either *one creature living* or *one was alive*.

In *The Making of Americans*, Stein stretches syntax almost to the breaking point and simultaneously limits her vocabulary. She says (pp. 539–40):

> To be using a new word in my writing is to me a very difficult thing. Every word I am ever using in writing has for me very existing being. Using a word I have not yet been using in my writing is to me very difficult and a peculiar feeling. . . . There are only a few words and with these mostly always I am writing that have for me completely entirely existing being.

Stein moves increasingly farther away from the concrete noun-centered vocabulary of the realistic novel. This is due partly to her subject matter. *The Making of Americans* is a monumental attempt to create a family chronicle to serve as an eternally valid history of all people, past, present, and future. "This is now a history of . . . every kind of men and every kind of women who ever were or are or will be living" (p. 220). In this book, Stein presents people as generalized types, using the novel's characters to represent all human possibilities. This leads her from the essentially conventional narrative that dominates the book's beginning to the generalized, theoretical digressions that are dispersed throughout the novel but are especially prominent toward the end.

The long passage cited earlier concerns David Hersland, but very little concrete information about him is supplied. Stein was trying to turn particular and perhaps personal facts (most critics consider the Hersland family to be autobiographical) into universally valid generalizations. This effort is reflected in the dearth of conventional nouns and the wealth of pronouns. This is a move toward obscurity: a pronoun's referent is more vague than a noun's. Neil Schmitz points out that in *The Making of Americans* neuter pronouns become increasingly frequent and distinctions between *he* and *she* disappear until "the massive coda of *The Making of Americans* lovingly relishes the indefinite pronoun: any one, some one, each one, every one."[40] Verbals replace conventional nouns and adjectives: *alive* becomes *being living*. The same phrase is also used as a noun: David Hersland is interested in *being living* rather than in life. This probably reflects Stein's desire to emphasize transitive linguistic processes over substantive ones in prose.

Participles, which prolong and de-emphasize whatever action is being described, replace conventional verbs. The participles contain very little concrete information. The passage under discussion contains five participles: *being*, *living*, *wanting*, *needing*, and *knowing*; but each is repeated a number of times. The least specific participlies are most often repeated; *being* and *living* each occur nineteen times in the paragraph.

Aside from the participles, few conventional adjectives are used in the passage. As for adverbs, *certainly* occurs a number of times here, as it does throughout the book. Perhaps this is Stein's attempt to reassure herself and the reader of the universal validity of her typology. Bridgman states: "Throughout the book tension is felt between those words that convey wholeness and assurance and those that express tentativeness. 'Completely' and 'certainly' must fight off the threatened encroachments of 'almost' and 'in a way.'"[41] And the fact that Stein must say "some," "many," and "a good deal" increasingly often may reflect her growing recognition of the limits of her undertaking. The adverb *then* is prevalent in the novel, perhaps related to Stein's attempt to bring all knowledge gained over time into the present moment, as she says in "The Gradual Making of *The Making of Americans*":

> When I was up against the difficulty of putting down the complete conception that I had of an individual, the complete rhythm of a personality that I had gradually acquired by listening seeing feeling and experience, I was faced by the trouble that I had acquired all this knowledge gradually but when I had it I had it completely at one time. . . . And a great deal of The Making of Americans was a struggle . . . to make a whole present of something that it had taken a great deal of time to find out, but it was a whole there then within me and as such it had to be said.[42]

The stylistic concerns of Stein's early prose, in both *The Making of Americans* and the early (pre-1912) portraits are extension of syntax and simultaneous circumscription of vocabulary, limited not merely in quantity of words, but also in the degree of specificity admitted. The result is a very vague and generalized portrayal of the subject matter. *The Making of Americans* fits Stein's requirements for prose very neatly. It is concerned with syntax and contains many verbs, adverbs, and conjunctions; it reduces the vocabulary and, for the most part, eliminates conventional nouns in favor of pronouns and gerunds. And naturally, a style that extends syntax will contain many connective words, such as prepositions and conjunctions.

It is interesting to compare Stein's prose style with Jakobson's observations of two kinds of obscurity found when one of the two basic linguistic operations is suppressed. Jakobson delineates two types of

obscurity, each related to a disfunction in one of the two linguistic axes
that Roland Barthes has termed *system* and *syntagm*. Jakobson refers to
these axes respectively as *selection* and *combination*:

> Any linguistic sign involves two modes of arrangement.
> 1) COMBINATION. Any sign is made up of constituent signs and/
> or occurs only in combination with other signs. This means that
> any linguistic unit at one and the same time serves as a context for
> simpler units and/or finds its own context in a more complex lin-
> guistic unit. Hence any actual grouping of linguistic units binds
> them into a superior unit: combination and contexture are two faces
> of the same operation.
> 2) SELECTION. A selection between alternatives implies the pos-
> sibility of substituting one for the other, equivalent to the former
> in one respect and different from it in another. Actually selection
> and substitution are two faces of the same operation.[43]

Some of Jakobson's observations about language produced when the
operation of selection is suppressed are similar to what is seen in the
prose style of *The Making of Americans* and the early portraits when
Stein *voluntarily* suppresses the operation of selection by severely limiting her vocabulary and attempting to eliminate nouns. Jakobson describes obscurity resulting from suppression of *selection* by saying that
"the more a word is dependent on the other words of the same sentence
and the more it refers to the syntactical context, the less it is affected"
when the operation of selection is suppressed. "Therefore words syntactically subordinated by grammatical agreement or government are
more tenacious, whereas the main subordinating agent of the sentence,
namely the subject, tends to be omitted." He goes on to note that "Key
words may be dropped or superceded by abstract anaphoric substitutes," and concrete and specific nouns and verbs may be replaced by
general words such as *thing* or *perform*. On the other hand, Jakobson
notes that "Words with an inherent reference to the context, like pronouns and pronominal adverbs, and words serving merely to construct
the context, such as connectives and auxiliaries, are particularly prone
to survive."[44] (It will be seen later, through some of Jakobson's observations, that obscurity produced by suppression of the second linguistic
operation—contiguity/combination—shares certain characteristics with
Stein's second style, which she called poetry).

It is important for Stein criticism that Jakobson's linguistic theories
are also applicable to nonverbal systems of signification. For example,
Jakobson suggests that a structural distinction between two kinds of
figurative language—metaphor (based on the operation of similarity)

and metonymy (based on the operation of contiguity)—be applied for the analysis of visual art:

> The alternative predominance of one or the other of these two processes is by no means confined to verbal art. The same oscillation occurs in sign systems other than language. A salient example from the history of painting is the manifestly metonymical orientation of cubism, where the object is transformed into a set of synecdoches; the surrealist painters responded with a patently metaphorical attitude.[45]

Jakobson's work can aid analysis of the two kinds of obscurity Stein produced in *The Making of Americans* and *Tender Buttons* phases, and in comparing those two kinds of verbal obscurity to the two kinds of visual obscurity produced during the analytic and synthetic phases of cubism. As has been suggested by Wendy Steiner and John Malcolm Brinnin, analytic and synthetic phases of cubism parallel stages in Stein's stylistic development as well.[46]

Gertrude Stein's patronage of cubism and of Picasso may be more widely known than her role as a writer. A brief look at the history of that famous friendship will precede a comparison between Stein's writing and Picasso's painting along the lines suggested by structuralist theory. Brinnin tells of Stein's first meeting with Picasso through art dealer Clovis Sagot:

> Gertrude met Picasso in 1905 at Sagot's, when she went there to inspect *Jeune Fille aux Fleurs*, which Leo was thinking of buying. Picasso happened to be in the gallery. When he saw Gertrude, he asked, "Who is the lady?" When Sagot identified her, Picasso said, "Ask her if she will pose for me," and retired to await an answer. When Gertrude accepted the proposal, their first shy meeting had already established a harmony that governed nearly all of their lifelong relations.[47]

The resulting *Portrait of Gertrude Stein* (1906) (Plate 1) took many sittings, and Gertrude Stein went daily to sit for Picasso in his rundown apartment in the Rue Ravignan:

> For perhaps eighty or ninety days through the winter of 1905–1906, she sat for him in a large broken armchair beside a cast-iron stove held together with wire and around which lay heaps of cinders and other pieces of crippled furniture. . . . But poverty was no hindrance to the association of souls as congenial and minds as lively as Picasso's and Gertrude's, and during the long series of

sittings for the portrait the foundations of their long, celebrated friendship were laid.[48]

Stein herself said that she talked her work over "endlessly" with Picasso during these sittings,[49] and the association between them did not end with the portrait's completion, but continued for forty-one years (interrupted occasionally by quarrels), as Mellow indicates:[50]

> In Picasso's studio or at the rue du Fleurus, they would sit, knee to knee . . . discussing the personal fortunes and habits of friends, the difficulties of their own work, their struggles, the state of the Parisian art world. Picasso had a fund of malicious observations about mutual acquaintances that Gertrude appreciated and remembered. He had, too, a way of summing up, in razor-sharp and emphatic statements, his ideas about art and the creative life that complemented and influenced her own way of thinking. When he told her, for example, that the artist who first creates a thing is "forced to make it ugly", that "those who follow can make of this thing a beautiful thing because they know what they are doing, the thing having already been invented, but the inventor because he does not know what he is going to invent inevitably the thing he makes must have its ugliness," she set it down as one of the larger truths to be gained from listening to a genius. It was to become a consoling dogma for her own creative efforts and her struggle to achieve the recognition she felt was properly due her own literary genius.
>
>   In trade for such insights, she might offer her own breath-taking generalizations, such as her belief that the reason she and Picasso were so responsive to each other was that they represented the most advanced and most backward of modern nations, America and Spain. They had, therefore, the affinity of opposites.[50]

What Gertrude Stein and Picasso discussed sitting "knee to knee" is a tantalizing, and probably unanswerable, question. But, according to Rogers, "She talked painting constantly with painters, critics, amateurs and the man in the street."[51] Picasso and several of the artists and painters who were his friends began to attend Stein's Saturday night gatherings.[52] But Gertrude Stein's friendship with Picasso was not limited to the Saturday night salons in her home. Leo and Gertrude bought many of Picasso's paintings when times were hard for him, as Mellow reports. Gertrude and Leo not only offered him hospitality and "bought the most lovely and difficult of his works," they also "displayed his works proudly, argued in his defense, and encouraged others to buy."[53] According to Rogers, when Leo and Gertrude first visited Picasso's studio, they invested eight hundred francs in his pictures, "a lot of money to invest in one artist in a city overflowing with them."[54] But as Picasso's work grew more extreme, Leo began to back away, favoring Matisse, Picasso's rival:

> Most of Gertrude's important new friendships were still shared with her brother, but gradually her creative needs brought her closer to Picasso and his circle and to relationships in which Leo had no part. While Leo continued to maintain good relations with Picasso, there was never any doubt that, in both his critical estimation and his affection, Matisse came first. . . . Leo looked suspiciously at anyone who operated principally on the level of intuition. Since Picasso believed that knowledge and intellect were dangerous things for an artist, there was very little common ground on which he and Leo could meet.[55]

It was Gertrude who continued in the role of benefactor and patron when "Leo's appetite for 'Cubist funny-business'" waned.[56]

In *Picasso*, Stein asserted that she alone understood him because she was doing the same thing in literature.[57] Leo Stein, in *Journey into the Self*, reported that Gertrude's portrait of Mabel Dodge "was directly inspired by Picasso's latest form."[58] According to Arnold Ronnebeck's sometimes contested reminiscence, Stein said, " 'Well Pablo (Picasso) is doing abstract portraits in painting. I am trying to do abstract portraits in my medium, words.' "[59] Stein never publically developed these analogies. But the strongest testimony that she did see such a relationship is the similarity between what she says of Picasso's work and what she says of her own work, as will be shown later. As for Picasso, he had little chance to know her works directly. Brinnin points out that "since he [Picasso] did not read English, he had no notion, except through hearsay, that she was his literary counterpart."[60]

To link Stein with the cubist painters often implies that she lacked originality and perhaps needed someone to lead her. If her brother Leo was no longer amiable, she could follow Picasso.[61] It is more likely that she did not find in the cubists a source for her ideas, but rather a group with similar concerns and perceptions about what art was and should be for the twentieth century. Like Stein, the cubists were interested in the process of direct perception. Stein saw in their work an affinity with some ideas she had been exposed to already, possibly in the pragmatism of William James.[62]

The fact that Stein often labeled her written works "portraits," "still lifes," and "landscapes" does not indicate naive effort to make "word pictures,"[63] but indicates a break with more commonplace literary forms.

In any case, Stein's first obscure style (prose) does, indeed, parallel the visual obscurity of analytic cubism.

Cézanne, of course, influenced both Gertrude Stein and the cubists. Stein said:

> Everything I have done has been influenced by Flaubert and Cézanne, and this gave me a new feeling about composition. Up to that time composition had consisted of a central idea, to which everything else was an accompaniment and separate but was not an end in itself, and Cézanne conceived the idea that in composition one thing was as important as another. . . . [T]hat impressed me enormously, and it impressed me so much that I began to write *Three Lives* under this influence and this idea of composition.[64]

Stein believed that until Cézanne the composition of a painting had a central figure and a background, but in Cézanne's work all things had equal importance. Stein described the cubist's composition as decentralized, with corners having as much importance as the center of the canvas: "not a composition in which there was one man in the center surrounded by a lot of other men but a composition that had neither a beginning nor an ending, a composition of which one corner was as important as another corner, in fact the composition of cubism."[65] In the cubist composition the positive space or figure explodes and scatters over what is traditionally negative space or ground. See, for example, Picasso's *The Accordionist* (Summer 1911) (Plate 7) and *Ma Jolie: Woman with Guitar* (Winter 1911–12) (Plate 8). Stein saw this as the composition of the twentieth century.

William Barrett has seen this decentralized "cubist" composition in twentieth-century literature as a whole. Barrett says the "flattening of pictorial space that is achieved in cubism" is paralleled in literature by "a general process of flattening," one aspect of which is:

> . . . the *flattening out of climaxes* which occurs both in painting and literature. In traditional Western painting there is a central subject located at or near the center of the picture, and the surrounding space in the picture is subordinate to it. . . . Cubism abolished the idea of the pictorial climax: the whole space of the picture became of equal importance. Negative spaces (in which there are no objects) are as important as positive spaces (the contours of physical objects). If a human figure is treated, it may be broken up and distributed over various parts of the canvas. . . . The spirit of this art is anticlimactic.[66]

Barrett sees this flattening of climaxes as the rejection of Aristotle's idea that a literary work must have a beginning, a middle, and end.

"No beginning, middle, end—such is the structureless structure that some modern literary works struggle toward; and analogously in painting, no clearly demarcated foreground, middleground, and background."[67]

Gertrude Stein's *Three Lives*, written in 1905–6,[68] is a roughly chronological narrative, without a sense of rising and falling action, because each episode is given equal weight. Because Stein wanted to capture the present moment, she soon rejected the conventions of beginning, middle, and end as not authentically representative of human perception of the world. "[I]f it is going to have a beginning and middle and ending it has to do with remembering and forgetting and remembering and forgetting is not interesting."[69] This led Stein to try to eliminate narrative from her portraits:

> When I first began writing . . . I naturally began to describe them [people] as they were doing anything. In short I wrote a story as a story . . . and slowly I realized this confusion, . . . that in writing a story one had to be remembering. . . . But . . . I wondered is there any way of making what I know come out as I know it, come out not as remembering. I found this very exciting. And I began to make portraits.[70]

These portraits reflect this new composition, which Stein based on Cézanne. In these static pieces, she no longer moves through time to tell a story as in *The Making of Americans*. Instead, each individual moment becomes important in itself. Each sentence is important, and no one sentence carries climactic meaning as in the traditional narrative. Instead, each sentence carries equal weight, emphasis, and information, as in this portrait of Matisse:

> This one was certainly a great man, this one was certainly clearly expressing something. Some were certain that this one was clearly expressing something being struggling, some were certain that this one was not greatly expressing something being struggling.
> Very many were not listening again and again to this one telling about being one being living.[71]

When Stein said she alone understood Picasso because she was doing the same thing in literature,[72] she was apparently referring to these portraits. Her analogy seems to have been made in the context of the development of "true cubism" (as she referred to it), which she dates as beginning in 1909 after Picasso's return from Spain.[73] She also refers to this period as characterized by the production of gray paintings,[74] meaning, of course, the era of analytic cubism (1909–12), when Braque and Picasso eventually eliminated all color except gray and ochre from their paintings.[75] There is an affinity between the analytic style of cubism and the style of some of Stein's literary portraits produced at about the same time, an affinity based on more than Cézanne's common influence on a new decentralized composition Stein called "the composition of cubism." The relationship between Stein's literary portraits and the portraits of analytic cubism becomes clearer when some of her other statements about her own early literary portraits, such as "Matisse" and "Picasso," are compared with her statements about Picasso's work.

Stein's statements imply that her portraits paralleled Picasso's in eliminating memory from perception; both wanted to preserve each individual present moment of perception before those moments are synthesized by intellectual knowledge of reality into the concept of the object as it is known (remembered) to be. The common influence of Cézanne is felt here in Picasso and Stein's shared interest in the process of perception over time. According to Fry, "Cézanne . . . had gone a step beyond the break with tradition represented by the impressionist's optical realism, to a realism of the psychological process of perception itself. Thus in painting Cézanne would . . . organize his subject according to separate acts of perception he had experienced; houses and other solid objects were depicted as the artist had conceptualized them after a long series of perceptions."[76]

In *Picasso*, Stein explains what Picasso was doing by saying that he knows faces as an infant does, one feature at a time, without organizing the many perceptions into a conceptual whole.

> A child sees the face of its mother . . . in a completely different way than other people see it. . . . the child sees it from very near, it is a large face for the eyes of a small one, it is certain the child for a little while only sees part of the face of its mother, it knows one feature and not another, one side and not the other, and in his way Picasso knows faces as a child knows them. . . . [N]o one had ever tried to express things seen not as one knows them but as they are when one sees them without remembering having looked at them.
>
> Really most of the time one sees only a feature of a person. . . . The other features are covered by a hat, by the light, by clothes . . . and everybody is accustomed to complete the whole entirely from their knowledge, but Picasso when he saw an eye, the other one did not exist for him and only the one he saw did exist for him and as a painter . . . he was right, one sees what one sees, the rest is a reconstruction from memory and painters have nothing to do

with reconstruction . . . with memory, they concern themselves
only with visible things.[77]

People learn to organize these perceptions in order to see objects.
This learned process is based on memory. Even when only one or two
facial features are visible, the adult reconstructs the rest from what he
remembers and knows from experience to be there. People may need
to see this way in order to organize the apparent sensory chaos of the
world into something that can be dealt with, but the cost is lessened
awareness of the isolated perception. Stein apparently saw that the cubists were presenting many individual perceptions of a subject without
consolidating them into a conceptual model.

In her lecture "Portraits and Repetition," Stein expresses her own
similar concern with the individual moment of perception, a preoccupation manifested in the phenomena that most call *repetition*. Stein's
repetition was based on a Heraclitean recognition that at each moment
both the perceiver and the object perceived change. She said of her
portraits, "I built them up little by little each time I said it it changed
just a little and then when I was completely emptied of knowing that
the one of whom I was making a portrait existed I had made a portrait
of that one."[78]

But Stein asserts that repetition is impossible; both the perceiver and
the entity perceived change from moment to moment, so there is always a difference in emphasis or "insistence."

> Is there repetition or is there insistence. . . . There is no such thing
> as repetition. And really how can there be . . . repetition . . . once
> started expressing this thing, expressing any thing there can be no
> repetition because the essence of that expression is insistence, and
> if you use emphasis it is not possible while anybody is alive that
> they should use exactly the same emphasis. . . . [79]

Stein says she created her portraits by writing down each perception in
isolation without reference to memory or past experience, that is, to the
mental concept of the person or object:

> Each time that I said that the somebody whose portrait I was writ-
> ing was something that something was just that much different
> from what I had just said that somebody was and little by little in
> this way a whole portrait came into being, a portrait that was not
> description and that was made by each time, and I did a great
> many times, say it, that somebody was something, each time there
> was a difference just a difference enough so that it could go on and

be a present something. . . . [I]n order to do this there must be no
remembering . . . remembering is also confusion.[80]

Stein also admired what she saw in Picasso's rejection of remembering:
"his attempts to express . . . not things remembered, not established in
relations but things which are there, really everything a human being
can know at each moment of his existence and not at all an assembling
of all his experience."[81]

Both Stein's first obscure style and analytic cubism reject past memory in favor of direct experience of the present moment. This use of
time is evident in the cubists' presentation of bits and pieces of a subject that changes each time one looks at it, then looks away to its image
on the canvas, then looks at the object again.[82] The cubists maintained
the multiplicity of viewpoints that results from such repeated moments
of looking without reconciling and consolidating them into a single
stable point of view. The result is fragmentation rather than traditional
renaissance perspective. Thus the attempt to bring all knowledge gained
over time into the present moment is common to both Stein's first obscure style and to analytic cubism.[83]

Steiner points out the similarity between the "non-mimetic relational
units" that make up the faceting of analytic cubism and "the first phase
of Stein's writing," which emphasized relational words. "The avoidance of nouns and adjectives and the abnormally frequent use of pronouns, copulars, adverbs and other shifters led to a purely relational
word unit."[84] Yet both Stein's early portraits and early cubist portraits
remained mimetic, evoking the subject by presenting a few bits of concrete information.

For both Stein and the cubists, the new composition inspired by Cézanne and the common interest in perception resulted in a uniformity
of "texture" —the repetition of uniform bits of visual information (color,
shape, line) or a uniform rhythm of repeated phrases, distributed rather
evenly (without climaxes) through the work as a whole.[85]

The repetitive, overlapping bits and pieces of minimal visual information presented in Braque and Picasso's work, as well as in Stein's
repetitive, overlapping sentences come from rendering isolated spurts
of perception, and from the presentation of parts rather than the whole,
a fact that Roman Jakobson recognized when he characterized cubism
as emphasizing the horizontal axis of language, the operation of conti-
guity/combination. In that cubism presents a series of synechdoches, it
is based on metonymy.[86]

The structuralists' delineation of two basic operations of language, selection and contiguity/combination, can illuminate the kinds of difficulties shared by Stein's reader and the viewer of cubist paintings, who are faced by two distinct types of obscurity. In that the spatial relationships on the picture plane deal with the arrangement of pictorial elements *in praesentia*, such concerns are based on contiguity or combination and thus involve the horizontal axis. This is most obvious in the traditional spatial relationships set up by perspective, which supplies information about the position of objects in relation to one another and to pictorial space. In language this information is supplied by prepositional phrases and prepositions, such as *in front of*, *in back of*, *above*, and *below*, words Jakobson associates with contiguity (the horizontal axis).[87] When cubists, following Cézanne's lead, dropped traditional perspective in favor of a new spatial syntax, their concern was still with contiguity and the horizontal axis. In analytic cubism, contiguity is emphasized, as the spatial configuration of the subject extends over the ground of the painting and the lines delineating the object are extended and realigned into segments that form small, overlapping planes which repeat similar configurations, as in Picasso's *Portrait of D. H. Kahnweiler* (1910) (Plate 2). In some ways this is similar to the extension of syntax in Stein's first obscure style.

Especially toward the end of *The Making of Americans*, the kernel of meaning of Stein's paragraph-sentence is distributed into repetitive[88] and overlapping clauses, each containing a minimal piece of the complete meaning.[89] Each clause ordinarily reproduces much of the information contained in the clauses that precede and follow it, although the word order may be rearranged, as in the following passage from *The Making of Americans* (p. 700):

> As I could be saying there are some living to be ones being good for living, there are some living to be ones making themselves and others good for living, there are some living because they are certain that there is some good to some one in their being living, there are some living certain that each one has some good in living, there are some living needing to be certain that sometime some one will be a good one.

The only difference between what Stein does here and what she does in her early portraits is she uses periods rather than commas in the portraits to separate her independent clauses.

The sentences of the portraits are often shorter than some of those in *The Making of Americans*. But the concern is still syntax, as the overlapping, repetitive sentences seem to coalesce into one long sentence among the many already long sentences that Stein still uses. Rather than trying to capture the slow growth of knowledge over time, she is now trying to capture each individual moment of knowing, and this is naturally reflected in her repetitive but somewhat shorter sentences. She also manipulates syntax as she recombines and reorders the elements in her basic vocabulary in each sentence, changing the meaning slightly each time, as in the following 1911 portrait "Four Dishonest Ones: Told by a Description of What They Do":

> She has been working, she is not needing to be changing. She has been one working and every one was knowing that she was not needing to be changing. She is what she is, she is not needing to be changing.
> She is one working. She is one not needing to be changing. She is one working. She is one earning this thing earning not needing to be changing. She is one not needing to be changing. She is one being the one she is being. She is not needing to be changing.[90]

Here Stein expands a kernel sentence into a number of varying surface structures.

Stein and Picasso share a desire to represent the integrity of the fleeting individual moment of perception before consolidation by memory into a conceptual whole. Both Stein's work circa 1909–11 and cubist painting produced at that time present an extremely slow, dispersed presentation of information normally presented much more quickly and held together as a conceptualization. This makes perception of subject matter in both Stein and Picasso difficult though not altogether impossible. Insistence on the individual present moment of perception makes it necessary for readers or viewers to use memory to hold the dispersed bits of information together to reconstitute the visually or verbally evoked image, if they try to do so. But the slowness of the presentation (in painting it takes the eye longer to see dispersed items than items placed close together) makes it very hard to do so. Thus both analytic cubism and Stein's first obscure style extend the spatial and temporal contiguity enough to force the perceiver to come to the work of art without memory, and to see the subject as "things seen not as one knows them but as they are when one sees them without remembering having looked at them."[91] Both emphasize the present tense, frustrating attempts to use memory to *read* subject matter.

Of course, critics have pointed out that the attempt to present the individual moment of perception works out quite differently in each medium. It is argued that in painting, the isolated fragments are seen almost simultaneously, and each bit of visual information remains on the canvas while the mind reconstructs the entity portrayed.[92] Reading goes much more slowly. Images are presented serially, and the entity portrayed appears less immediately than in a painting. Strother B. Purdy wrote:

> Even if a rapid reading rate is supposed, it cannot be said that Gertrude Stein's images pass before the eye faster than one every two or three seconds. It is impossible to see them, therefore, as "not many things but one thing," since we perceive them separately, and the perception can be as boring as being shown even the most thrilling film at the rate of one frame every three seconds.[93]

Stein's images have a cumulative, rather than simultaneous, effect. Ironically, then, memory *is* necessary to apprehend her subject matter from the slow presentation of miminal bits of information, if one insists on reconstituting the conceptualized whole, rather than seeing the individual parts (which is probably the wrong way to read Stein).

In any case, the resulting monotony is perhaps an even greater cause of difficulty in reading Stein than the obscurity itself. The reader may disagree with Stein that "remembering is confusing," and may feel that the stymieing of memory by repetition makes her writing fail as literature. Whether in prose or poetry, memory has traditionally played a key role. In prose the story is built up over time, and the reader must remember events in sequence to follow the story. In poetry visual and/or aural memory of rhythm and rhyme, as well as meaning, lend continuity and coherence to the work and, in fact, define the work as a poem, at least in traditional thinking.

Stein's rejection of memory may have a negative impact on many readers, but it also reflects Stein's philosophical premises, as will be shown later in this chapter. Similar problems result from the emphasis on present tense in cubism, but aren't as severe in painting, because one may perceive the parts more quickly and may perhaps enjoy the individual visual configurations more than is possible with the individual word or sentence in Stein's writing.

Many critics have said that Stein's work resembles that of Picasso and Braque in its movement toward abstraction. This is true if by *abstraction* one means *the opposite of concrete*. But the aims of analytic cubism were not abstract in the sense of nonrepresentational. During those early years, Stein, Braque, and Picasso were still concerned with fidelity to an entity outside their work, to the referent. But the nature of their interest led them toward abstraction. Harold Rosenberg said: "In regard to the object . . . cubist painting was involved in a contradiction: it wished to dissolve objects into directly apprehended forms — the stem and bowl of a pipe glimpsed separately—yet it wished to preserve the objects themselves as presences."[94] The cubists wanted to paint the underlying reality of things as they really are, rather than as people think they see them. To reach that essential reality, the cubists eliminated detail and simplified forms. Although most lines and planes in cubist paintings refer only to spatial relationships (a concern with contiguity and therefore with the horizontal axis of language), the desire to hold onto the object is evident in the lines descriptive of hair and hands, for example, in Picasso's *Portrait of D. H. Kahnweiler* and *Portrait of Wilhelm Uhde*.

Stein, too, was interested in the essential reality of her subject. She eliminated narrative and physical description to achieve a perception of the "bottom nature" of the person. Bridgman states that: "By selecting general nouns and verbs, and replacing nouns with pronouns that lacked distinct referents and if possible, gender—'one' and 'some'—she moved steadily towards abstraction."[95] But, of course, one can only say that Stein moved *toward* abstraction. It is not possible to achieve through words the same level of abstraction that can be achieved through lines and planes. Words always call up concepts; the signifier and signified always coexist. (Whether or not the same is true of lines is problematic.)[96]

For both the reader of Stein's work produced circa 1909–11 and the viewer of a Picasso painting produced at about the same time, the problems of obscurity are compounded by suppression of the operation of selection. In both cases, the signifying elements available (for Stein, vocabulary; for Picasso, plastic elements such as color and tone) are severely limited. Just as Stein's substitution of pronouns for nouns and vague, indefinite verbs for action verbs made meaning obscure, Picasso's limited choice of colors, tones, and lines makes his paintings harder to "read." (Both Stein and Picasso demand of the audience an active role in "reading" the work.) The suppressed vocabulary of pictorial elements eliminates cues that normally allow the subject matter to be easily read. Color and texture, traditionally mimetic of the object painted, cannot approximate that descriptive function when limited to grays and ochres and uniform brush strokes, and when lines are limited to certain stylized geometric configurations. Robert Rosenblum says, "The vocabulary, too, is increasingly austere, approaching an ascetic reduction to straight lines and clean-cut arcs . . . which, by 1910, will result in an almost completely geometric representation of . . . the human body."[97]

Tones and values that usually aid the reader in seeing depth in a painting are limited to a middle range. Not only does this elimination of light and dark tones make the painting's depth necessarily shallower, it also makes it ambiguous and harder to read, as in Picasso's *Portrait of a Woman* (1910) (Plate 9), *Female Nude* (1910–11) (Plate 10), and *Man With A Pipe* (1911) (Plate 11). In any case, in Stein's literary portraits of the participial style, there is what Fry called "an unapprehended subject behind the opaque surface of the prose"[98] just as there is in analytic cubism a barely perceptible presence behind the opaque or translucent surface of lines and planes. Despite its apparent "abstraction," Stein's portrait of Picasso conveys a hint of his energy and playfulness:

> This one was one who was almost always working. This one was not one completely working. This one was one not ever completely working. This one was not one working to have anything come out of him. This one did have something having meaning that did come out of him. He always did have something come out of him.[99]

The concern here is still representation; the work is not totally abstract. (Picasso was always working, but this work was always very close to play. He achieved meaning without apparently working toward that as a goal.)

Thus the concern of Stein's first obscure style (the prose of both *The Making of Americans* and of the early portraits) is still mimesis. The style is somewhat abstract (as opposed to concrete), but these works as a whole are not abstract because each attempts to mirror reality.

WITH *Tender Buttons* Stein made a radical change from the prose style of *The Making of Americans* and other early works to a style that she called poetry. From prose, with its emphasis on syntax and its suppression of vocabulary, she moved to poetry, with its emphasis on vocabulary and suppression of syntax. This change was manifested by shifting emphasis from the linguistic operation of combination (horizontal axis) to the operation of selection (vertical axis).

Tender Buttons did attain "a certain notoriety" in the press and attract polemical criticism, perhaps because it does seem to "veer off into meaninglessness," at least in conventional terms.[1] But it is more than a literary curiosity. The stylistic change it marks was a breakthrough that influenced the direction of much of Stein's future work. As Bridgman says, "For Gertrude Stein, *Tender Buttons* represented her full scale break out of the prison of conventional form into the colorful realm of the sensitized imagination."[2] It marked a change from mimesis of external reality to mimesis of the intersection of the present moment of consciousness with an object. It also marked the emergence of her "literature" as a piece of independent reality, as a thing in itself with no need to represent any other objective reality to justify its existence.

In *The Making of Americans* Stein's concerns were imposing order upon the world by classifying people into universal, eternally valid types, creating a history of all human possibilities. This called for language that expressed generalities very precisely. Stein's attempts to show a person's "bottom nature," the essence beneath the apparent particularity, continued in her early portraits. Bridgman says:

> Gertrude Stein had tried numerous techniques in her previous efforts to match her conception of a person with a style. She had generalized and reduced her vocabulary in order to make true statements, however simple-minded. She had constructed long, cumulative sentences on the model of This-is-the-house-that-Jack-built to convey the feeling of slowly becoming familiar with a person.[3]

But by the time Stein wrote *Tender Buttons*, her attention was no longer focused on the universals of experience, but rather on the process of experiencing each moment in the present tense as it intersects with consciousness. In *The Making of Americans*, she had subordinated particularity and individual differences to the type. But she eventually abandoned this approach, as Sutherland points out: "But by rejecting her knowledge of types, Gertrude Stein was faced with each experience as a unique thing, with even its importance unprejudiced, as simply different."[4] Stein had simplified and generalized reality to impose order upon it, but finally she had "concluded that greater fidelity of representation might be achieved if she simply recorded the verbal responses her consciousness made to a particular subject, while minimizing her own manipulation of them."[5]

In her lectures (written with many years' hindsight, which perhaps gave her stylistic development more coherence than it really had), Stein discusses her new desire to see the world and return to the sensual particularity of experience immediately available to consciousness. After writing her portraits, she slowly became bothered by the fact that she was leaving out looking at the world. "So I began to do this thing, I tried to include color and movement, and what I did is . . . a volume called *Tender Buttons*."[6]

The Making of Americans, with its historical orientation and its quasi-scientific goal of classifying people according to type, necessitated remembering the past. Classification is based on resemblances, on similarities, which must be remembered. In her early portraits, Stein freed herself of narrative and presented perceptions one moment at a time. But these perceptions were not dealt with "in the raw." They were edited, selected, and generalized so that the person could be analyzed and

presented in his or her essential reality. But in *Tender Buttons* Stein
came to terms with the chaotic nature of real experience and with what
Bridgman calls "the existential swarm of her impressions."[7] The physical world is experienced as unique and immediate in each present moment as the consciousness receives data.

In any discussion of Stein's writing, the word *abstract* is bound to
come up. Too often the term *abstract*, when used to describe Stein's
writing, is taken to mean *nonrepresentational*, and her writing almost
never is nonrepresentational. She never really abandons subject matter.
In her early work the subject matter was the representation of types of
people or of particular people, which led to interest in the process of
perception itself. In the style *Tender Buttons* exemplifies, the subject
matter is the intersection of the object with consciousness. As attention
becomes focused on the process of perception, that process becomes as
much a part of the subject matter as the object perceived. Stein said,
"As I say a motor goes inside and the car goes on, but my ultimate
business as an artist was not with where the car goes as it goes but with
the movement inside that is of the essence of its going."[8] In fact, Stein
insisted on subject matter and disapproved of abstract art. Leon Katz
and Edward Burns quote Stein as saying, " 'The moment art becomes
abstract, it is pornographic.' "[9] That the cubists' work was never abstract, i.e., never nonrepresentational, is not always clearly understood
by those who compare Stein's writing with the work of those painters.
But as Robert Rosenblum points out in *Cubism and Twentieth Century
Art*, neither analytic nor synthetic cubism is completely divorced from
the subject matter.

> It is certainly true that many Synthetic Cubist drawings and paint-
> ings after 1912 offer a capricious rearrangement of reality that would
> be impossible in the Analytic phase. However, it must be stressed
> that this presumed independence of nature is more often of degree
> than of kind. . . . [T]he post-1912 works of Picasso, Braque, and
> other Cubists often depend on as close a scrutiny of the data of
> perception as did the pre-1912 works, however different the results
> may seem. Without this contact with the external world, Cubism's
> fundamental assertion that a work of art is related to but different
> from nature could not be made; for there would be no means of
> measuring the distance traversed between the stimulus in reality
> and its pictorial re-creation.[10]

Subject matter is certainly not abandoned in *Tender Buttons*; neither,
as Bridgman puts it, does that book "signal an abandonment of control.
Her practice was to concentrate upon an object as it existed in her
mind. . . . Gertrude Stein perceived that it [the object] was immersed

in a continuum of sound, color and association, which it was her business to reconstitute in writing."[11] In *Tender Buttons* the subject matter is not limited to description of the objective world; it also includes the intersection of the real world with the writer's consciousness. As Weinstein explains, description in *Tender Buttons* "consists of a moment in the subjective continuum of the writer that corresponds to the moment of visual perception of the object."[12] Weinstein, in defining *linguistic moment*, states: "Each second of experience has its corresponding moment in mental time. And in any second of mental time there are words, both in and out of sequence. I would suggest that we call this linguistic cluster in any moment of mental time the 'linguistic moment.'"[13] What Stein represents in *Tender Buttons* then is this linguistic moment in the writer's consciousness. "In that moment, the words that came to Miss Stein's mind were disjointed, disembodied, unassociated, not the conventional descriptive words associated with the object in everyday discourse."[14]

But one *can* say the vocabulary of her early writing moves toward abstraction, if by that one means it moves away from the concrete, is very general, and contains few concrete nouns and verbs of action: "He was one being living, then when he was quite a young one, and some knew him then and he knew some then. He was one being living then and he was being one and some knew he was that one the one he was then and some did not know then that he was that one the one he was then." (*The Making of Americans*, p. 852.) *Tender Buttons* has a less abstract vocabulary in that it contains many more concrete nouns, sensual adjectives, and action verbs than does her earlier style: "The stove is bigger. It was of a shape that made no audience bigger if the opening is assumed why should there not be kneeling. Any force which is bestowed on a floor shows rubbing. This is so nice and sweet and yet there comes the change, there comes the time to press more air. This does not mean the same as disappearance" (p. 64). This passage contains a more concrete vocabulary than a typical passage from *The Making of Americans*: concrete nouns such as *stove, audience, opening, kneeling, floor, rubbing, time*, and *air*; adjectives such as *bigger, nice*, and *sweet*; and action verbs *comes* and *press*. However, in a different sense *Tender Buttons* is more abstract than *The Making of Americans*, because its words are used plastically, arbitrarily, and because it is less concerned with traditional discursive description.[15] Thornton Wilder said:

In the previous centuries writers had managed pretty well by assembling a number of adjectives and adjectival clauses side by side; the reader "obeyed" by furnishing images and concepts in his mind and the resultant "thing" in the reader's mind corresponded fairly well with that in the writer's. Miss Stein felt that that process did not work any more. Her painter friends were showing clearly that the corresponding method of "description" had broken down in painting and she was sure that it had broken down in writing. . . . Miss Stein felt that writing must accomplish a revolution whereby it could report things as they were in themselves before our minds had appropriated them and robbed them of their objectivity "in pure existing." To this end she went about her house describing the objects she found there in the series of short "poems" which make up the volume called *Tender Buttons*.[16]

As the concerns of Stein's writing gradually shifted from orderly analysis of the world to the immediate perception of the world by the consciousness, her writing dealt increasingly with the word itself: with mental images called up by and associated with words (signifieds), and with the qualities of words as things in themselves (signifiers). Bridgman said, "Her imagination was stimulated then not by the object's particular qualities alone, but also by the associations it aroused, . . . and by the words as they took shape upon the page."[17]

Perhaps coincidentally, a similar shift in emphasis was occurring in cubist painting around the time *Tender Buttons* was composed.[18] The earlier struggle in analytic cubism to see reality without the conventional, learned trompe-l'oeil of perspective focused the cubists' attention on the elements of composition and led them to realize that the artist could use these elements of composition arbitrarily as well as mimetically. Douglas Cooper, in *The Cubist Epoch*, points out that:

> . . . in the winter of 1912–13 a fundamental change came about in the pictorial methods of the true Cubists. Whereas previously Braque and Picasso had analyzed and dissected the appearance of objects to discover a set of forms which would add up to their totality and provide the formal elements of a composition, now they found that they could begin by composing with purely pictorial elements (shaped forms, planes of color) and gradually endow them with an objective significance.[19]

Cooper also says that the cubists had arrived at "the conclusion that they could create their own pictorial reality by building up towards it through a synthesis of different elements."[20] That elements of signification (forms, colors, textures) might have importance in their own right and that the artist could use them arbitrarily to create not a mirror of reality but an authentic new reality—the work of art as *tableau-*

objet—was an important realization for the cubists. Stein was aware of this change. In *Picasso*, she indicates that after 1912 the lines which had replaced the cubes "were more important than anything else, they lived by and in themselves. He painted his pictures not by means of his objects but by the lines."[21] Stein evidently arrived at a similar conclusion about words and literature, perhaps independently.

In terms of Stein's writing, this realization was that words need no longer be merely the means to the expression of another reality, but may become freed of their normal mimetic function (while still retaining their meanings and associations) and be used plastically by the writer. In her lecture "Portraits and Repetition," Stein describes her growing concern with the quality of language as a thing in itself:

> I began to wonder at . . . just what one saw when one looked at anything. . . . [D]id it make itself by description by a word that meant it or did it make itself by a word in itself. . . .
> I became more and more excited about how words which were the words that made whatever I looked at look like itself were not the words that had in them any quality of description. . . .
> And the thing that excited me . . . is that the words . . . that make what I looked at be itself were always words that to me very exactly related themselves to that thing . . . at which I was looking, but as often as not had as I say nothing whatever to do with what any words would do that described that thing.[22]

Like the cubists, Stein abandons conventional description of the object, though she is still concerned with the object as her "model." But she inverts the traditional descriptive relationship of word to object. Rather than the word evoking the mental image of the object, the object evokes words (e.g., associations) that the writer arbitrarily assembles into an independent linguistic object related to, but not descriptive of, the model or referent.

In analytic cubism, the artist abstracts forms from the given object and creates a representation of it (however unconventional) on canvas. In synthetic cubism, forms have their genesis in the artist, although he may use them to create an object on the canvas, as in Picasso's *Guitar and Wine Glass* (1912) (Plate 5) or Braque's *Still Life with Pipe* (1912) (Plate 12). Edward Fry, in *Cubism*, points out that after 1911 the cubists "no longer worked from a model in nature," but instead created "an ideational notation of forms that were equivalent to objects in the visual world without in any way being illusionistic representations of those objects."[23] Although the painting's visual ties to the real world supply much of its meaning and tension, its function is no longer to represent or describe that reality but to exist as a thing in itself.

In Stein's early work (*The Making of Americans* and other works of her participial style) words are used to abstract generalities about the world and analyze or describe them on paper. Words in *Tender Buttons* are not conventionally descriptive of the object but originate in the writer and in the sensual and/or linguistic associations evoked by the object. The writing no longer exists merely to describe the given object but becomes an entity in its own right. Steiner states that Stein, in her second phase, *also* created the kind of "ideational notation" suggested by Fry.[24]

In *Tender Buttons*, with the new attention to the immediately present moment and the abandonment of traditional description, Stein turned from her earlier "portraits" of people to the treatment of inanimate objects, and felt some bond with the painters of still lifes. In "Portraits and Repetition," Stein said that dealing with human beings "inevitably carried in its train realizing movements and expression and as such forced me into recognizing resemblances, and so forced remembering and in forcing remembering caused confusion of present with past and future time." So, instead of producing chiefly "portraits of men and women and children," she began to produce "portraits of rooms and food and everything because there I could avoid this difficulty of suggesting remembering more easily . . . than if I were to describe human beings."

Stein felt she shared this problem with the painters: "I began to make portraits of things and enclosures . . . because I needed to completely face the difficulty of how to include what is seen with hearing and listening and at first if I were to include a complicated listening and talking it would be too difficult to do. That is why painters paint still lives. You do see why they do."[25] Indeed, as they turned from analysis of a given reality on canvas to synthesis of a new reality from the pictorial elements, for a time the cubists (especially Picasso) produced fewer portraits and more still lifes. Perhaps the reason for this change is the same for both Stein and Picasso: dealing with inanimate objects allows the artist more freedom to treat the subject arbitrarily. In *Picasso* Stein points out that "Most people are more predetermined as to what is the human form and the human face than they are as to what are flowers, landscapes, still lifes."[26] The public expects a portrait to be a likeness of the model, whose face has the annoying habit of appearing in public, allowing itself to be compared with the painting. But a still life is a small piece of reality that the artist arranges arbitrarily and dismantles when he is finished, leaving the public nothing to compare the painting with.

In synthetic cubism the realization that pictorial elements could be used arbitrarily was marked by a return to color and texture from the predominantly gray paintings of analytic cubism. Cooper points out that "By the summer of 1912 . . . Braque and Picasso had made of Cubism a language in which they were not only able to recreate forms, volume and space in a new way, but which they were at last beginning to enliven with small passages of color and textural variations."[27] The beginnings of this return to color can be seen in the small patches of bright blue, yellow, and red in Picasso's *Violin, Glass, and Pipe on Table* (1912) (Plate 13), in the strong blues in Braque's *Still Life with Pipe* (1912) (Plate 12), and in the colored pictures of fruit in Picasso's *The Violin (Violin and Fruit)* (1913) (Plate 17).[28] The return to texture can be seen in the painted wood grain in Picasso's first *papier collé*, *Still Life with Chair Caning* (1912) (Plate 4) and in the painted wood grain and fabric in Braque's *Oval Still Life* (*Le Violon*) (1914) (Plate 14), and even plaster in Picasso's *Violin and Guitar* (1913) (Plate 15). Stein points out that during "his last period of pure cubism, that is to say from 1912–1917,"[29] Picasso began to enjoy "decorating his pictures,"[30] which became "more and more brilliant in color."[31] The color is applied arbitrarily or decoratively rather than descriptively. Textures also are used to provide interest rather than to describe objects. For example, see Picasso's *Green Still Life* (1914) (Plate 6) or *Still Life with Chair Caning* (Plate 4).

For Stein the new interest in sensory experiences of the present moment and the new freedom in using words were manifested in a richer, more sensual vocabulary, which contrasts with the spare, spartan vocabulary of her earlier work. Bridgman says "The idea had entered her mind that lyricism contained a fuller measure of truth than could ever be encircled by making endless, laboriously deliberate statements."[32] The evocative power of the word called for a more "decorative" approach. Freed from concerns with generalizing and classifying, Stein began to concentrate on the present moment and all the phenomena therein, including the words called up by those phenomena and their effect upon her conscious mind. So, instead of the genderless pronouns, verbs of being, prepositions, and conjunctions and the virtual elimination of concrete words in her earlier style, there is a renaissance of the particular: concrete nouns, sensual adjectives, and specific verbs.

This new concrete, decorative vocabulary appears not only in *Tender Buttons*, but in other works produced at the same time, such as "The

Portrait of Mabel Dodge at the Villa Curonia," as the following passage illustrates: "Gliding is not heavily moving. Looking is not vanishing. Laughing is not evaporating. There can be the climax. There can be the same dress. There can be an old dress. There can be the way there is that way there is that which is not that charging what is a regular way of paying. There has been William. All the time is likely."[33] The Mabel Dodge portrait is almost as significant as *Tender Buttons* in the development of Stein's stylistic shift. It is a transitional work, which combines the expanded vocabulary of her second style with some of the repetition of her first style. The passage cited above contains many concrete nouns, adjectives, and verbs: e.g., *gliding, moving, looking, vanishing, dress, old, paying, William,* and *time.* The syntax resembles that of her early portraits, but it is not yet fragmented as it will be in *Tender Buttons.*

The Dodge portrait is also important in tracing Stein's relationship to cubism. Bridgman dates Stein and Toklas's visit to Mabel Dodge's Villa Curonia (during which this portrait was written) as fall of 1912.[34] This is only a few months after Picasso began to use collage in May 1912, which led to synthetic cubism.[35] It is this work of Gertrude Stein that Leo Stein reports to have been directly influenced by "Picasso's latest form."[36]

This new interest in the word itself—in the noun especially and the word's associative powers—was what Stein considered the essence of poetry. In *Tender Buttons* and other works that Stein labeled *poetry,* the chief linguistic operation is association and word choice, variously labeled by structuralists as *substitution, selection,* and *system.* The association of words and concepts by similarity or opposition and the selection of a word from a group of synonyms are operations involving the vertical axis of language. Interestingly, the *Tender Buttons* style suppresses syntax (the horizontal axis) while it expands vocabulary. Syntax becomes increasingly fragmentary, disappearing altogether in some of the more extreme passages.

In *The Making of Americans,* the chief stylistic interest is syntax. But in *Tender Buttons,* the central concern is diction, the selection of words based on association, on the basis of either similarity or opposition. The long sentence-paragraph is abandoned, as more attention is focused on the noun. Stein writes:

After I had gone as far as I could in these long sentences and paragraphs . . . I then began very short things . . . and I resolutely realized nouns and decided not to get around them but to meet them, to handle in short to refuse them by using them and in that way my real acquaintance with poetry was begun.[37]

> . . . I began to discover the names of things, that is, . . . to discover the things . . . to see the things to look at and in so doing I had of course to name them not to give new names but to see that I could find out how to know that they were there by their names or by replacing their names. . . . They had their names and naturally I called them by the names they had and in doing so having begun looking at them I called them by their names with passion and that made poetry . . . it made the Tender Buttons.[38]

However, as Stein abandons extension of the sentence and enriches diction, the result is not more conventional writing but rather a new style that is as obscure as her earlier style, if not more so, and even harder to read in the traditional sense.[39] This obscurity is frequently due to disjunction between the two operations of language. The words *selected* may be similar in terms of sound or sense but do not *combine* with each other syntactically, semantically, or grammatically. "There is a way to see in onion and surely very surely rhubarb and a tomato, surely very surely there is that seeding" (*Tender Buttons*, p. 40). Sometimes one word seems unrelated to the others in the sentence except in terms of their existence as pure words (grammatical structure, rhyme, or wordplay). For example, the words in the following sentence are linked chiefly by alliteration and grammar: "The settling of stationing cleaning is one way not to shatter scatter and scattering" (p. 12).

Of course, words can't be divorced from their meanings. Each word (signifier) calls up a mental image or idea (signified). But, as Perloff put it, "[W]ords, as even Gertrude Stein recognized, have meanings, and the only way to MAKE IT NEW is not to pretend that meaning doesn't exist but to take words out of their usual context and create new relationships among them."[40] Thus one cannot read *Tender Buttons* or works like it with the conventional concern for subject matter because the total configuration of these mental constructs can't be used to mentally reconstruct the "subject matter."

Sometimes a *Tender Buttons* sentence may have normal syntax and orthodox grammar, yet the words selected don't relate to each other in a traditionally discursive way. "The change of color is likely and a difference a very little difference is prepared. Sugar is not a vegetable" (p. 9). These sentences are grammatically correct despite omission of conventional punctuation. One feels that the sentence would be perfectly comprehensible if the context were supplied. Stein uses both syntax and diction, but because of the disjunction between the two axes of language, the sentence does not "mean" in a conventional way.

Sometimes Stein explores patterns of language in *Tender Buttons*, repeating syntactical patterns while arbitrarily inserting terms from the pool of associated words in her vocabulary. "Almost very likely there is no seduction, almost very likely there is no stream, certainly very likely the height is penetrated, certainly certainly the target is cleaned. Come to sit, come to refuse, come to surround, come slowly and age is not lessening" (p. 70). She explores the rhythm and patterns of speech that are present even when discursive meaning is not. Like jabberwocky, this passage conveys the feeling of speech even though the words do not relate to each other in a conventional way.

In *Tender Buttons*, sentences become shorter, as the emphasis shifts from syntax to diction and association. In a lecture Stein explains that the lines of poetry are shorter than those of prose, because

> such a way to express oneself is the natural way when one expresses oneself in loving the name of anything. Think what you do . . . when you love the name of anything really love its name. Inevitably you express yourself . . . in the way poetry expresses itself that is in short lines in repeating what you began in order to do it again. Think of how you talk to anything whose name is new to you a lover a baby a dog or a new land. . . . Do you not inevitably repeat what you call out and is that calling out not of necessity in short lines.[41]

Often in *Tender Buttons* lines that appear to be sentences are not sentences. "Cutting shade, cool spades and little last beds, make violet, violet when" (p. 54). This fragment promises to be a sentence until it is truncated after the word *when*, which normally is used to introduce a subordinate clause. The disjunction between diction and syntax creates false predication. How can shade, spades, and beds *make violet*? Here each word is quite independent of those preceding and following it in the speech chain, at least as far as the mental images or signifieds are concerned. (Obviously, however, there are relationships between some of the words in terms of sound—the rhyme in *shade* and *spade*, for example, and the repetition of the long *a* in *shade*, *spade*, and *made*.)

Stein uses punctuation in other ways to break up the continuity of the sentence. "This makes an eddy. Necessary" (p. 54). Or "Cream cut. Anywhere crumb. Left hop chambers" (p. 55). She carries the disintegration of syntax even further, presenting a list within the horizontal structure of the sentence. (A list usually groups items associated with one another because they are similar in some way.) "Alas a doubt in case of more to go to say what is cress. What it is. Mean. Potatoes. Loaves" (p. 54). Here Stein plays wordgames with *more* and *less* (suggested by *more* and *cress*). She also associates *mean* and *potatoes* (substituting *mean* for *meat* by changing one letter) and possibly also suggests *meat loaves* instead of *mean loaves* on first reading. The association of cress with all this food is quite logical. The use of lists of words, seen in the above passage, later became more common in Stein's work. As will be shown in chapter 3, she eventually abandoned syntax in some works and used lists of words or phrases in vertical columns.

Again some of the stylistic phenomena of Stein's second obscure style, which emphasizes vocabulary and the noun while suppressing syntax, are strikingly close to Jakobson's observations about language produced when continguity/combination is suppressed and syntax disappears, leaving only isolated words. Jakobson states that when the operation of combination, "the ability to propositionalize or to combine simpler linguistic entities into more complex units" is suppressed, the result is not wordlessness: "There is no wordlessness, since the entity preserved in most of such cases is the word, which can be defined as the highest among the linguistic units compulsorily coded, i.e. we compose our own sentences and utterances out of the word stock supplied by the code."[42] Instead, what results is a diminution of "the extent and variety of sentences" as "The syntactical rules organizing words into a higher unit are lost; this loss, called AGRAMMATISM, causes the degeneration of the sentence into a mere 'word heap.'" "Word order becomes chaotic; the ties of grammatical coordination and subordination . . . are dissolved. As might be expected, words endowed with purely grammatical functions, like conjunctions, prepositions, pronouns, and articles, disappear first, giving rise to the so-called 'telegraphic style,'" whereas when the operation of similarity/selection is suppressed, the " 'kernel subject word' is the first to fall out of the sentence."[43] Stein's emphasis on the word and her deliberate disintegration of the sentence would logically follow if she is indeed deliberately suppressing what we now call the operation of combination.

Structuralist distinctions between the linguistic operations of combination (continuity) and selection (similarity) illuminate the relationship between Stein's second obscure style, represented by *Tender Buttons*, and synthetic cubism. In synthetic cubism, selection is stressed. The vocabulary of signifying elements is no longer constricted as in analytic cubism. There is a fuller use of color and texture, as in Picasso's *Guitar and Wine Glass* (1913) (Plate 5) in which pieces of pasted paper add color (blue and orange) as well as the patterns of wallpaper, woodgrain, and newspaper print to the painting. However, as in Stein's second obscure style, the relationship between signifying element and subject matter may be tenuous. For example, in Picasso's *Guitar and Wine Glass*, colors and textures are used arbitrarily rather than realistically or descriptively. Part of the guitar is bright blue, and part is covered with wallpaper. Color and texture are no longer tied to the object but are entities in their own right, to be used freely for compositional purposes without concern for their naturalistic occurrence.[44] Signifying elements such as color and texture, which normally act as cues allowing the subject matter to be "read," are present again. But the style is obscure anyway because these cues often contradict their traditional meanings. Color isn't even necessarily limited to the drawn outline of the object to which it is applied. In Picasso's *Man with a Hat* (December 1912) (Plate 16) a human face is made of newspaper. This is certainly a nonnaturalistic use of texture and pattern. Lines, as Stein pointed out, have become important in themselves and function primarily to delineate arbitrary shapes and only secondarily, if at all, to describe objects.

While selection is extended in synthetic cubism, as in Stein's second kind of obscurity, combination (contiguity) is suppressed. All cubist art implies a tension between the two-dimensional picture plane and the three-dimensionality of space represented. But, whereas analytic cubism with its spatially complex faceted surface seems to place more emphasis on a shallow three-dimensionality, synthetic cubism emphasizes the surface of the picture plane, sometimes in a very witty reminder to the reader that the depth in a painting is an illusion (as in Braque's famous trompe l'oeil nails painted on the surface of the painting). The emphasis on the painting's flat surface, first produced in collage by pasting flat pieces of paper on the picture plane, suppresses relationships of spatial syntax by de-emphasizing depth. Spatial syntax seems to refer more to the picture plane (left, right, up, and down) than to the depth of illusionistic space, as it does in the more complex spatial syntax of traditional perspective. Or, more accurately, synthetic cubism *does* refer to traditional expectations of illusionistic space only to playfully negate them by making these relationships ambiguous, just as Stein's second style constantly refers to conventional grammatical syntax, but only in a playful negation of its every rule.[45]

As in Stein's second obscure style, the signifying elements selected may work against the spatial syntax rather than with it. As modeling is generally eliminated, colors are flattened and so emphasize the relative absence or ambiguity of depth. Tone is no longer restricted to a middle range as in analytic cubism, but despite this, is no longer a cue for depth perception, as in Picasso's *Guitar and Wine Glass* (Plate 9). Lines do not clarify spatial relationships by providing perspective. Depth becomes ambiguous as relationships of *in front of*, *behind*, *forward*, and *back* become impossible to read. In *Guitar and Wine Glass*, it is hard to tell if one is looking *through* the guitar at a wall or if the wall is part of the guitar. Actually, all such questions are no longer relevant. We are looking at an opaque surface, not through a window on the world. Stein's second obscure style and synthetic cubism both force attention on the signifying element as a thing in itself and on the art object in its own right as an opaque surface—of paint and pasted paper or of words— to be looked *at* rather than *through*.

Attention to the signifying element for its own sake is closely tied in Stein's mind to poetry, which is what she called this second obscure style, which suppressed syntax and emphasized vocabulary.[46]

In *Tender Buttons* the prime concern is words and their associations. Stein's selection of words often seems motivated by a spirit of love and play. She says: "Poetry is concerned with using with abusing, with losing with wanting, with denying with avoiding with adoring with replacing the noun. . . . Poetry is doing nothing but losing refusing and pleasing and betraying and caressing nouns."[47] Sometimes in *Tender Buttons* selection of words is obviously related to the object:

A PETTICOAT.
A light white, a disgrace, an ink spot, a rosy charm [p. 22].

The associations between word and object are fairly obvious here. Petticoats are lightweight and often white, a petticoat showing or stained with an ink spot is a "disgrace" and might provoke a modest blush, "a rosy charm." (Gertrude Stein has been greatly overread, but it seems safe to identify the obvious and public associations.)

Even when the relationships of word to object are chiefly based on associated meanings, similarities of spelling and sound may play a role:

A METHOD OF A CLOAK.
A single climb to a line, a straight exchange to a cane, a desperate adventure and courage and a clock . . . all makes an attractive black silver [pp. 13–14].

The "single climb to a line" might relate to the shape of the cloak. The cane is linked to the cloak as an object of apparel. (Both the cane and the cloak have a nostalgic, perhaps nineteenth-century flavor of elegance.) But the two phrases *A single climb to a line* and *a straight exchange to a cane* also have identical rhythmic patterns as well as assonance (*straight, exchange,* and *cane*) and near rhyme (*climb* and *line*).[48] The "desperate adventure" and "courage" might be connotations connected to "cloak and dagger." Black may be the color of the cloak, which is attractive; silver was perhaps evoked by sight of the cloak's lining and the associated phrase *silver lining. Clock* may be associated with *cloak* because of similarity in spelling and sound.

In Stein's association of mental constructs (signifieds), she uses association based on both contiguity—defined by James as association of objects habitually found together in time and space, and identified by Jakobson as metonymy—and on similarity—which Jakobson identifies as metaphor.[49] Both kinds of association are operations of selection that function along the vertical axis of language. The metaphorical association predominates in *Tender Buttons*, which is what one might expect given Jakobson's observation that metaphor is absent when similarity is suppressed and metonymy is absent when contiguity is suppressed.[50] The operation of association is stressed not only in images and concepts (signifieds), but also in the qualities of the words as words (signifiers).

Stein often plays with the word as a thing in itself in *Tender Buttons*, and she chooses words because of their associations with other words as signifiers.[51] For instance, she often uses rhyme within the line, "all the joy in weak success, all the joyful tenderness, all the section and the tea, all the stouter symmetry" (p. 35). Similarly:

CHICKEN.
  Alas a dirty word, alas a dirty third alas a dirty third alas a dirty
  bird [p. 54],

and "The sister was not a mister" (p. 65).

She also associates words on the basis of alliteration: "The sight of a reason, the same sight slighter, the sight of a simpler negative answer, the same sore sounder, the intention to wishing, the same splendor, the same splendor, the same furniture" (p. 12). She even uses onomatopoeia:

CHICKEN.
  Stick stick call then, stick stick sticking, sticking with a chicken
  [p. 54].

Play with sounds and meanings of words leads to puns. Another similarity Steiner sees between "Stein's second phase" and synthetic cubism—is their "polysemous" quality—Stein's use of puns and the condensation of signs for objects in cubism. "The pun functions in the same way in Stein's writing, as do Stein's beloved 'mistakes,' combining a number of possible referents or a number of different aspects of the same referent into a single sign."[52] The following passage contains puns, evoking associations of Washington, wellington, and veal Wellington:

VEAL.
Very well very well, washing is old, washing is washing [p. 53].

More punning appears in the following:

MILK.
Climb up in sight climb in the whole utter needless and a guess a whole guess is hanging. Hanging, hanging [p. 47].

Stein even plays with the spelling of words: "and easy express e.c." (p. 55). Finding puns in Stein's work can be a pleasant occupation. Steiner has even uncovered a number of French/English puns in Stein's writing. However, the danger in carrying this occupation too far will be discussed in chapter 6.

The devices Stein uses in her "poetry" are certainly traditional (or at least they seem so now): indirect associations of imagery, obliqueness, fragmented syntax, rhyme, rhythm, and alliteration. What is it, then, that so many have found upsetting? Perhaps it is the lack of discursive meaning or the fact that the "subject matter" cannot be reconstructed from the words and images like a jigsaw puzzle. But these expectations may be inappropriate for Stein's writing.

Ironically Stein's intention in writing *Tender Buttons* was to capture immediate experience as consciousness grapples with it; but there have been many problems in reading the book. One difficulty caused by the text is the disjunction of the two axes of language, which makes it almost impossible to read the work for conventional discursive content. This problem leads to yet another problem: the effort of trying to figure out or reconstruct the content not only exhausts readers but overdistances them from the work itself. Such effort is futile anyway, for *Tender Buttons* demands to be dealt with on its own terms. Stein gives the reader none of the literary allusions that Pound, Eliot, or Joyce give. As for inventing glosses for the little pieces in *Tender Buttons*, Sutherland points out that it is possible and amusing to create them, but that "it is perfectly idle."

Such a procedure puts the original in the position of being a riddle, a rhetorical complication of something rather unremarkable in itself. It would be rather like an exhibition of the original table tops, guitars, pipes, and people which were the subject matter of cubist paintings. The original subject matter is or was of importance to the painter as a source of sensations, relations, ideas even, but it is not after all the beholder's business. The beholder's business is the picture in front of him, which is a new reality and something else, which does not add up to the nominal subject matter.[53]

As Sutherland suggests, what the reader of Stein must do is also look *at* the work rather than *through* it. The reader can't look through it because it is a flat and opaque rather than deep and transparent style. If one does look *at* the work, what does one see in *Tender Buttons*? One sees the word presented as an entity in its own right. By forcing the reader to pay attention to the word, Stein makes the word seem new again. Stein doesn't ignore the meanings of words, as so many critics alleged. But by presenting each word in an unusual context, she directs attention not only toward its sound but also toward its sense, as the reader is forced to grapple with each word one at a time. The reader must confront the word and language itself with a sense of bewilderment, wonder, and discovery. Stein says in "Poetry and Grammar": "Nouns are the names of anything and anything is named, that is what Adam and Eve did and if you like it is what anybody does, but do they go on just using the name until perhaps they do not know what the name is or if they do know what the name is they do not care what the name is. . . . And what has that to do with poetry. A great deal I think. . . ."[54] Poetry's role, then, is to rejuvenate and revitalize the word: "you can love a name and if you love a name then saying that name any number of times only makes you love it more, more violently more persistently more tormentedly. Anybody knows how anybody calls out the name of anybody one loves. And so that is poetry really loving the name of anything. . . ."[55]

Stein's fascination with language, both sound and sense, and her interest in exploring its way of working certainly shows in *Tender Buttons*. Her possibly intuitive grasp of the principles of its operation is evident not only in her theories, but also in the very nature of the two so very different kinds of obscure styles she created.

2. Pablo Picasso, *Daniel Henry Kahnweiler*, 1910. 39⅝ × 28⅝″.
COURTESY OF THE ART INSTITUTE OF CHICAGO.

3. Pablo Picasso, *Portrait of Wilhelm Uhde*, 1910. 31⅞ × 23⅝".
COURTESY OF JOSEPH PULITZER, JR. PHOTOGRAPH BY DAVID GULICK.

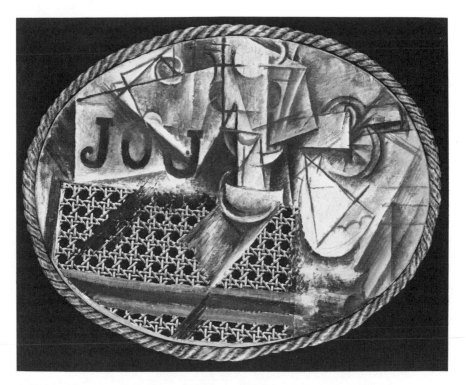

4. Pablo Picasso, *Still Life with Chair Caning*, 1912. 27 × 35″.

5. Pablo Picasso. *Guitar and Wine Glass*, 1912. 18⅞ × 14⅜″.
MARION KOOGLER McNAY ART INSTITUTE, SAN ANTONIO, TEXAS.

6. Pablo Picasso, *Green Still Life*, 1914. 23½ × 31¼".

7. Pablo Picasso, *The Accordionist*, 1911. 51¼ × 35¼".
THE SOLOMON R. GUGGENHEIM MUSEUM, NEW YORK.
PHOTOGRAPH BY ROBERT E. MATES.

8. Pablo Picasso, "*Ma Jolie*," 1911–12. 39⅜ × 25¾″.

9. Pablo Picasso, *Portrait of a Woman*, 1910. 39⅜ × 31⅞".

10. Pablo Picasso, *Female Nude*, 1910–11. 38¾ × 30⅜".

11. Pablo Picasso, *Man with a Pipe*, 1911. 35¾ × 27⅞″.
COURTESY KIMBELL ART MUSEUM, FORT WORTH, TEXAS.
PHOTOGRAPH BY BOB WHARTON.

12. Georges Braque, *Still Life with Pipe*, 1912. 13¼ × 16⅜".

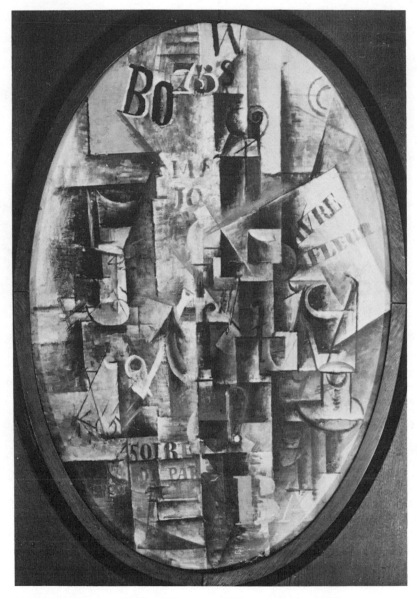

13. Pablo Picasso, *Violin, Glass, and Pipe on Table*, 1912.
31⅞ × 21¼″.

14. Georges Braque, *Oval Still Life (Le Violon)*, 1914. 36⅜ × 25¾".
COLLECTION, THE MUSEUM OF MODERN ART, NEW YORK.
GIFT OF THE ADVISORY COMMITTEE.

15. Pablo Picasso, *Violin and Guitar*, 1913. 36 × 25″.

16. Pablo Picasso, *Man with a Hat*, 1912. 24½ × 18⅝″.
COLLECTION, THE MUSEUM OF MODERN ART, NEW YORK. PURCHASE.

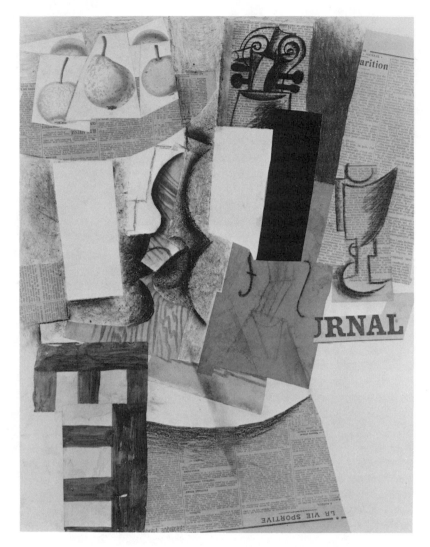

17. Pablo Picasso, *The Violin (Violin and Fruit)*, 1913. 25½ × 19½".

SYNTAX ABANDONED:

THE LIST IN STEIN'S PLAYS, POEMS, AND PORTRAITS

ALTHOUGH THE CUBIST CIRCLE was disrupted by World War I, Stein's association with Picasso was not.[1] But developments in Picasso's work after the shift to the synthetic phase are not paralleled in Stein's work. Stein and Picasso individually developed those ideas generated in the earlier cubist epoch, but without direct influence on each other except through the residual influence of that earlier era. As Picasso and Stein moved independently in separate directions, Stein's stylistic innovations, perhaps growing out of her earlier cubist associations, continued to develop. While Picasso continued to increase his pictorial vocabulary by adding still more color and texture to his paintings, Stein, on the other hand, continued to suppress syntax and stress the individual word, eliminating the sentence in favor of the list in some of her writing.

Stein's increasing destruction of syntax and emphasis on diction, first developed in *Tender Buttons*, eventually resulted in her recurrent abandonment of the visually and linguistically horizontal format of the sentence. The complete elimination of syntax, the use of columns of words and phrases, and the use of the list as a generating and structural principal of Stein's works were preoccupations that recurred throughout the rest of her career. Weinstein claims that conventional syntax is based on a perception of the world as orderly. In the truncated and even destroyed syntax here, Stein continues her attempt to come to terms with the world as chaotic, immediate, and unordered experience, which is how she felt life is perceived. In *Tender Buttons* she merely truncates sentences into fragments, while keeping the visual appearance of prose: the horizontal format of the sentence and the paragraph.

> CHICKEN.
> Alas a doubt in case of more to go to say what it is cress. What is it. Mean. Potato. Loaves [p. 54].

But eventually abandoning the sentence and the paragraph, she instead organizes words or phrases in columns down the page without syntax.

Stein's increasing suppression of syntax by vertical columns and lists of words in her post-1912 plays, poems, and portraits is an extreme variation of her second obscure style. This style emphasizes the individual word even more than *Tender Buttons*, which is written in paragraph form. But this use of lists, like the use of language in *Tender Buttons*, is based on an extended vocabulary and suppressed syntax. It was similarly classified as poetry by Stein's definition, often occurring alongside paragraphs resembling the *Tender Buttons* style.

Richard Bridgman dates Stein's first use of the list as occurring in 1912 in "Monsieur Vollard et Cézanne":

> For the first time in her career, Gertrude Stein placed single words, phrases and sentences in vertical columns. . . . The consequence was that her word play was emphasized as had never been possible when it was crowded into a paragraph. The possibilities struck her as attractive. As she finished the piece . . . she signalled her awareness of the novelty. "Yes I have gotten a new form."[2]

The use of lists and columns appears throughout her career, and is quite strong especially before the late thirties. (In the mid-thirties Stein returns to a horizontal format in a new prose style that incorporates elements of this vertical style, as will be seen in chapter 4.) So in Stein's last play, *The Mother of Us All*, written in 1946, there are still vestiges of the tendency to use columns of words and phrases even though the columns are short and appear in a text largely made up of dialogue presented in paragraphs:

Thaddeus S.	Be mean.
Daniel Webster.	Be there.
Henrietta M.	Be where.[3]

Weinstein sees Stein's suppression of syntax as a challenge to the conventional way of seeing the world serially rather than simultaneously:

> [S]imultaneity is the experience of sensing two or more mental phenomena simultaneously in any one given moment of consciousness. As Marshall McLuhan notes in *The Gutenburg Galaxy* it is precisely this experience of simultaneity that literature on the printed page threatens. The meaning of any group of words that comprise a sentence on a printed page is limited to the meaning the typography imposes upon the words. In other words, the meaning of any sentence is the meaning as derived from the sequential, left-to-right collection of discrete units of information. The acceptance of sequential unit by unit, semantic synthesis of the discrete units is the act of comprehending the printed sentence.[4]

So by eliminating syntax Stein was challenging not just grammatical structure, but also thought processes and discursive logic conventionally expressed as a horizontal written record of the discourse. She not only questions chronological order and substitutes simultaneity for seriality, but challenges the basic structure of prose. What Michel Butor has to say about prose may explain the implications of Stein's vertical rather than horizontal structures. For Stein attention to the present moment led to abandonment of chronological order; and Butor, in "The Book as Object," points out that the conventions of reading a book from beginning to end, left to right, and top to bottom lose their validity once chronological order is rejected.

> Once our eyes are open, we can see that this misconception of the book as an object of consumption like food was in fact possible only with regard to a certain category of works which the habits of criticism and of literary history force us to consider as the only important as well as the largest one, which is far from the case, i.e., those works which are in effect the transcription of a discourse running from start to finish of the *volumen*, narrative or essay, and which it is therefore natural to read by starting them on the first page in order to finish them on the last, thus constituting the time span of a hypothetical "hearing." It is obviously only in this case that one may act as if the first lines were fading, vanishing, as one reaches the last ones. But most of the books we use are not created in this fashion. We do not generally read them all the way through; they are reservoirs of knowledge from which we may draw, and which are arranged so that we can find as easily as possible the information we need at a given moment. Such are

dictionaries, catalogues, manuals, tools indispensable to the functioning of a modern society, the books most read, most studied; and if, quite often, they have only a slight literary value, so much the worse, of course, for us.[5]

By suppressing the sentence, Stein also attacks the conventional way of seeing and conceptualizing the world. Weinstein points out: "Our syntax, our ways of combining words, is grounded in Aristotelian logic — a logic that made considerable sense at the time of its inception and makes less sense every century since. A linguistic logic based upon laws of direct causality and linear time cannot authentically correspond to a universe of possibilities such as James describes."[6] *Tender Buttons*, which attacks the sentence by fragmenting it and "scrambling" its syntax, to use Weinstein's term, also challenges the logical Aristotelian way of looking at the world and substitutes a new way of seeing, which is basically the way of William James. "In *Tender Buttons* the Jamesian universe of flux and process is dramatized by the processual syntax; the description, the verbal embodiment of the object, is as plastic, as multidimensional and as protological as objective reality itself."[7]

Stein's vertical columns attack the paragraph—a unit of sustained thought—as well as the sentence. Even in works largely made up of columns of words, sentences and sentence fragments are still dispersed throughout. But even when several sentences occur together in a column, they do not coalesce to form an organic unit. Instead each sentence becomes a unit in a random list of phrases and sentences, none of which is related very strongly to what precedes and follows, as in the following passage from "Have They Attacked Mary He Giggled," written in 1917:

PAGE VIII

Can you speak.
The dog.
Can you bear to tear the skirt.

PAGE IX

Lighting.
We can see the lighting.

PAGE X

Can a Jew be wild.

PAGE XI

A great many settlers have mercy. Of course they do to me. You are proud. I am proud of my courage.[8]

Earlier, in *The Making of Americans*, Stein had extended the paragraph to portray duration. But here the paragraph disintegrates as she focuses on time as a series of individual moments during which consciousness intersects with the object, rather than as a slow process of coming to terms with knowledge.

This new vertical format appears increasingly often as Stein creates works or parts of works that suppress syntax almost totally. For example, "Oval" (1914) is written almost completely as a column of words and short phrases:

> Needles.
> Package.
> No whatever.
> Ever so much.
> Thank you.
> Suddenness.
> Excellent.
> Utensils.[9]

The use of very conventional phrases, such as *Ever so much* and *Thank You*, as in the above quotation, is very common in Stein's writing. Rogers points out that many of Stein's famous and often used phrases come from riddles and childhood games.[10] Weinstein calls this use of "Snips, or cutups from every day conversation" taken out of context the " 'cut-up' method."[11]

Such conventional phrases really function as one-word items in a series. Because they are ready-made phrases, there is no combinative operation to be performed; the combination of words in the phrase is already fixed by convention. The speaker or writer selects the entire phrase rather than the individual words. Barthes calls such phrases "fixed syntagms" and quotes Saussure's statement that " 'there is probably also a whole series of sentences which belong to the language, and which the individual no longer has to combine himself."[12] Jakobson also states that "In any language there exist also coded word-groups called PHRASE-WORDS. The meaning of the idiom *how do you do* cannot be derived by adding together the meanings of its lexical constituents; the whole is not equal to the sum of its parts. Word-groups which in this respect behave like single words are a common but nonetheless only marginal case."[13]

Stein's frequent use of phrase-words, such as *Thank you* and *Ever so much* as in the passage above from "Oval," is found in many of her "vertical" works. For example, "An Exercise in Analysis," written in

1917, contains the phrases *Can you forgive me*,[14] *Thanks so much*,[15] *Yes indeed* and *Of course you do*,[16] and *Thank you*.[17]

In these columns virtually total emphasis is on selection, with minimal emphasis on combination. Here the word, isolated and independent of syntax, is the primary concern, as words, phrases, and sentence fragments are merely arranged in columns down the page. This is evidence of an emphasis on the individual word in isolation that is even heavier than in *Tender Buttons*. Stein discusses her discovery of the impact of the isolated word: "I found that any kind of book if you read with glasses and somebody is cutting your hair and so you cannot keep your glasses on and you use your glasses as a magnifying glass and so read word by word makes the writing that is anything something" (*The Geographical History of America*, p. 150). Interest in isolated words emphasizes word choice (selection) associated with the vertical axis of language. These columns of words suppress syntax (combination) associated with the horizontal axis even more than does *Tender Buttons*, which retains the horizontal format of prose. In "The Book as Object," Michel Butor points out in a section called "Horizontals and Verticals":

> The narrative, the essay, whatever might form a discourse heard from beginning to end, is transcribed in the West on a horizontal axis running from left to right. This, as we know, is merely a convention. Other civilizations have adopted others.
>
> The two other dimensions and directions of the volume—from top to bottom for the column, from nearer to farther for the pages— we generally regard as quite secondary in relation to the first axis. All the links usually studied by grammar are established along this dynamic horizontal, but when we encounter a certain number of words which have the same function in the sentence, a series of direct objects, for example, each one is attached in the same fashion; they have basically the same position in the sequence of links, and I perceive a kind of interruption in the line's movement; this enumeration is arranged, then, perpendicular to the rest of the text.
>
> If I express this perpendicular typographically, everything will be clearer; I will then, so to speak, "factor out" the grammatical function of all these terms.[18]

As noted before, poetry often subordinates syntax to diction, and modern poetry sometimes suppresses syntax entirely. Stein, defining poetry as concerned with the noun rather than the sentence, felt that enumeration of names of objects made for poetry. In the lecture "What Is English Literature," she says,

As I say description of the complete . . . daily island life has been England's glory. Think of Chaucer, think of Jane Austen, think of Anthony Trollope, and the life of the things shut up with that daily life is the poetry, think of all the lyrical poets. . . . They have shut in with them in their daily island life . . . all the things that just in enumeration make poetry, and they can and do enumerate and they can and do make poetry, this enumeration.[19]

As the poetic line grows shorter, obviously the ultimate result is the one-word, even one-syllable, line, which makes the poem look like a column.

> My Gay.
> Baby.
> Little.
> Lobster.
> Chatter.
> Sweet.
> Joy.
> My.
> Baby.[20]

This column of words, enclosed by the phrases *Dear Jenny.* and *Be Good./Always.* resembles a love letter, underscoring Stein's idea that poetry is that loving wordplay based on the noun, an idea Stein discusses in her lecture "Poetry and Grammar."

Similarly, the drama is very easily adapted to the vertical format. Although many Stein plays are written as a series of short paragraphs in which sentences are truncated as in *Tender Buttons*, many of her plays contain passages in which the line of dialogue is shortened to one or two words. In her lecture "Plays," Stein said: "Poetry connected with a play was livelier than poetry unconnected with a play. In the first place there were a great many bits that were short and sometimes it was only a line."[21] This series of short lines forms a vertical column, as in Stein's opera *Four Saints in Three Acts*:

> Saint Therese.   When.
> Saint Settlement.   Then.
> Saint Genevieve.   When.
> Saint Cecile.   Then.
> Saint Ignatius.   Then.[22]

The typographical arrangement of most of her plays usually creates two columns, one made of the characters' names and the other made up of lines they speak. Here she keeps the spacing between the two items constant. Another typical layout is to line up all the names of the characters in one column, and all the lines spoken in another column, with the left-hand margin kept constant in both cases.

Bridgman also links columns of words to Stein's discovery of the play. "The formal resemblance of such an arrangement to dialogue did not escape Gertrude Stein."[23] Neither poetry nor drama is tied to the paragraph as prose is, and both lend themselves easily to emphasis on the vertical axis and suppression of the horizontal axis of language. In a play the utterance is usually relatively short. Characters rarely sustain the chain of speech for more than a few paragraphs, except in an extended monologue. In most cases dialogue is an exchange of one- or two-sentence speeches. As Bridgman points out, the vertical arrangement does seem conducive to the use of dialogue (relying heavily on *very* short phrases or even one-word lines).

Weinstein points out that Stein often creates dialogue in her plays with "Snips, or cutups from everyday conversation."[24] The more conventional and ready-made the phrase, the less the writer has to use the operation of combination. The shorter the line of dialogue, the more the play approaches a vertical format. In 1932, Stein even created a play made up of lists of short lines, and called it *Short Sentences*:

Henry Winter.	It is most.
James Ferguson.	Which is for them.
Arthur Prentiss.	All of which is for them
Jane Heap.	All of which
John Randolph	Is for them
Nelly Mitchell.	But which she will[25]

But in any case, even the most conventional play contains lists: lists of characters (in order of appearance or importance, separated into groups of males and females). Stein, who was interested in this kind of list, says that when she read Shakespeare's plays "it was always necessary to keep one's finger in the list of characters for at least the whole first act, and in a way it is necessary to do the same when the play is played."[26]

The main structure of the play can also be thought of as a list of scenes and acts that take place in numerical (chronological) sequence, and the dialogue can be seen as a list of lines spoken in a particular sequence. Gertrude Stein parodies this structure in her play *Listen to Me*, written in 1936:

| Fourth Act. | Of course |
| Fourth Act. | The air |

Fourth Act.	Is full
Fourth Act.	Of it
Fifth Act.	And Sweet William
Fifth Act.	And his Lillian
Fifth Act.	Tell me[27]

Stein plays with and against all of these conventional lists within the structure of the play. Dramatic content often seems subordinated to exploiting the printed script's potential for creating vertical patterns.

One way in which Stein does this is by toying with the conventional lists of characters, as she does in many of her plays. In *Four Saints in Three Acts* she mimics the convention of separating characters into two lists, male and female, at the beginning of the play. She creates two similar lists in *Four Saints* and even places them directly before the beginning of a section called Act One:

Saint Theresa	Saint Ignatius
Saint Matyr	Saint Paul
Saint Settlement	Saint William
Saint Thomasine	Saint Gilbert
Saint Electra	Saint Settle
Saint Wilhelmina	Saint Arthur
Saint Evelyn	Saint Selmer
Saint Pilar	Saint Paul Seize
Saint Hillaire	Saint Cardinal
Saint Bernadine	Saint Plan
	Saint Guiseppe[28]

Here Stein plays with and against conventional assumptions about lists by imposing an artificial similarity on what is basically a random series. The names are not listed in any particular order. Since real and spurious saints are mixed, similarity is not a consistent basis for association. But by putting the title *Saint* before each name, Stein imposes an artificial similarity on the items listed. Names of real and fictitious saints are mixed together, as are French, Latin, German, Spanish, and Italian names.

The conventional format of the play first identifies the character and then provides that character's line of dialogue. Stein seems to use both the names of characters and the lines themselves largely as a pretext for making lists. For example, at one point in *Four Saints in Three Acts*, the names of the characters are important for the sake of creating a kind of catalog. It would be impossible for the audience to identify so many individual characters, some of whom have no lines to speak.

Saint Settlement
Saint Chavez   How much of it is finished.
Saint Plan
Saint Therese.
Saint Therese.   Ask how much of it is finished.
Saint Chavez.   Ask how much of it is finished.
Saint Therese.   Ask how much of it is finished.
Saint Settlement
Saint Therese
Saint Paul
Saint Plan   Ask how much of it is finished.
Saint Anne
Saint Cecile
Saint Plan.[29]

This list goes on for two pages. The only obvious purpose of so many characters is to call attention to this enumeration of names. There surely couldn't be a serious dramatic function for so many characters.

Stein also turns the conventional dramatic dialogue into a list of short phrases. In some Stein plays, the character speaks so many separate successive lines with the dialogue tag repeated that Stein's interest in creating a list seems stronger than her interest in creating a dramatic structure. For example, in *They Must. Be Wedded. To Their Wife.* she writes:

Therese.   Crowned in glory.
Therese: Crowning glory.
Therese.   Trained Therese.
Therese.   With them with seen.
Therese.   With lace.[30]

This continues for twenty lines. In conventional drama a twenty-line speech by a character is usually presented in paragraph form, and the dialogue tag is never repeated for each line or sentence. Perhaps Stein is implying that one becomes a different character at each successive moment of one's existence. But a more obvious objective of this technique is avoidance of the sentence and the paragraph, which are units of sustained discourse about a particular idea.

A play like *Short Sentences* supplies an enormous number of characters, again at least in part to emphasize the vertical format, since the audience will obviously not be able to remember and identify so many characters by name. Neither could so many speaking parts conceivably be necessary to the plot.

Albert Lincoln.	Should much
Edith Lorer.	As very likely
Mabel Earle.	Just why they rose.
Abel Melcher	Just if they thought
Ruth Winfield.	Just why they left.
Edith Henry.	Making it be right[31]

This list of characters continues for fifteen pages without apparent repetition of any names. The audience cannot remember the characters
well enough to care about them or relate them to the plot, and so must
come to terms with the play as an immediate spectacle.

Stein uses the numerically ordered structural divisions of the play not
to enhance the plot but to play games with such a rationally ordered
series. Sometimes she deliberately makes each act or scene extremely
short (one or two lines), making it obvious that a play is really a *list* of
lines spoken or read within a circumscribed list of segments—scenes
or acts—presented in chronological order.

Part II.
Act I.

Believe in your mistake.

Act II.

Act quickly.

Act III.

Do not mind the tooth.

Act IV.

Do not be careless.[32]

In this play, Stein follows normal chronological and numerical order of
play's parts, but that is not at all the rule in Stein's plays. For example,
in *A Play of Pounds* she writes:

Act I Scene two
Should make it do or did she hear me.

Scene one

For this how are ours fortunately.

Act II

It is thought that they were never careful

Scene one

Indeed they must have been given to be pleased with
care for it.

Scene two

Our acceptance.

Scene one and scene two
For more or for more of for acceptance[33]

Here act 1, scene 2, precedes scene 1; and act 2 has two first and two second scenes. Stein rejected chronological order in most of her works because it involves memory, which she found confusing, and because it is based on the old-fashioned assumption that things happen in logical progression. Perhaps Stein's emphasis on the vertical format of drama encouraged her to look at the structural and visual appearance of the play, in print as well as onstage, rather than at traditional concerns. Plot, with its beginning, middle, and end, distracts attention from the present moment and involves remembering. And emphasis on character leads to the sort of emotional reaction to a play that Stein believed detracted from the play as a spectacle (or "landscape") rather than as a drama.

So, as one would expect, it is in Stein's poems and plays that the recurrent disintegration of the sentence in favor of a column of words most often occurs. Sometimes the column of words contains a real sentence presented in a vertical format, as in "Study Nature," written in 1915:

I
Am
Pleased
Thoroughly
I
Am
Thoroughly
Pleased.[34]

But, more often, although the word order is appropriate for a sentence, the potential sentence has been divided into several one- to three-word fragments separated by periods and arranged in columns down the page:

Please leave slippers.
For me.[35]

She even cuts fragmentary phrases into still smaller pieces:

The long life.
Of Mabel Digsby.
The youth.
Of Henry the Eighth.[36]

Total obliteration of syntax is quite often found in Stein's lists, as she creates what Jakobson called a "word heap," i.e., vocabulary without syntax, which occurs with the suppression of the linguistic operation of combination. This "aggrammatism" or word heap, which results when syntax is suppressed, may occur along with some "one-sentence utterances and one-word sentences. Only a few longer, stereotyped, 'ready-made' sentences manage to survive."[37] When Stein consciously does away with syntax, she also occasionally makes a word heap. Sometimes this occurs in a horizontal format. Although written horizontally across the page, the following group of words is not a sentence though it might look like one; it lacks subject and verb and really has no syntax per se. "MABEL, MARTHA AND MABEL AND MARTHA: Susan Mabel Martha and Susan, Mabel and Martha and a father."[38] This word heap cannot be a sentence because it is constructed entirely of nouns and conjunctions. It *really* is a list of names. As Butor points out in "The Book as Object," a list can be presented horizontally. "An enumeration, a vertical structure, can be introduced anywhere in a sentence; the words which compose it can have any function, as long as it is the same one. They may even occur outside a sentence."[39] Such an enumeration can be a sentence only if subject and verb are attached to it, so that the list itself functions as a direct object (extended, of course) or a predicate nominative. (I went to the store to buy eggs, milk, cheese, bread, and butter.)

Stein's list above contains a set of persons, but the following word heap appears much more random:

BANKING

Coffee, cough, glass, spoon, white, singing. Choose, selection, visible, lightning, garden, conversation, ink, spending, light space, morning, celebration, invisible, reception, hour, glass, curving, summons, sparkle.[40]

This is an even more extreme example of a word heap. For one thing, the words are not all the same part of speech; although most of them are nouns, the series also contains verbs. There are some logical relationships: *coffee* and *cough* are related by their similar sound, whereas *coffee*, *glass*, and *spoon* are associated by contiguity (i.e., they are items usually thought of as belonging together in space and time). However, there doesn't seem to be any principle of order or similarity maintained throughout. Here Stein plays *against* the convention that all the words in a list should have a common denominator. She supplies just enough links to suggest that the association is meaningful, then she teases the reader by not sustaining the principle of the association.

The word heap occurs most often in vertical format.

When.
When in.
Iron.
Oat.
Labor.
And.
Opera.
Opera coat.
Coat.
If a.
Stamp.[41]

Although it often seems that Stein has created a completely chaotic group of words, this is not always true. The above examples are actually *lists* of words. Butor points out that lists can be "open or closed," "amorphous or structured."[42] This format, which abandons not only syntax but even the visual semblance of the sentence, is most characteristic of Stein's almost total emphasis on selection and the vertical axis of language, which began with the horizontal lists found in *Tender Buttons* and grew more extreme. The first two sections in *Tender Buttons* are really lists: the first, of objects—a box, a plate, a seltzer bottle—(pp. 14–16); the second, of foods—rhubarb, single fish, cake, and custard (pp. 50–51).

Sometimes the list may even function as the organizing principle of a work, as in "To Do: A Book of Alphabets and Birthdays."[43] Donald Gallup, in the introduction to *Alphabets and Birthdays*, points out that its structure is based on "an orderly progression through the letters of the alphabet with four names for each letter."[44] For example, the narrative for the letter *a* begins:

Everything begins with A.
A. Annie, Arthur, Active, Albert.
Annie is a girl Arthur is a boy Active is a horse. Albert is a man with a glass.[45]

The alphabet is a list, and Stein adds a horizontal narrative to each item of that list. Butor points out that "Just as enumerative vertical structures may occur within horizontal structures (sentences), so horizontal structures can be attached to the items in a list; this is what happens in all dictionaries or encyclopedias."[46] This is also the basis of the structure of "To Do: Alphabets and Birthdays." However, Stein more often creates vertical lists of single words; and even though the list combines words without syntax, the association and ordering of the words are often based on some principle operative in list-making.

Even the construction of a list on a principle of randomness is based on another kind of order. For example, items may be associated by a principle of random selection, such as a list of names chosen from the telephone directory by some arbitrary means. All the items in such a list have in common the fact that they were selected in the same way. What makes Stein's use of the list often disconcerting, however, is that sometimes even a principle of randomness is not sustained throughout, thus dashing the reader's expectations even in that regard. Stein both affirms and parodies rational principles that are the basis of list-making. For example, in "If I Told Him: A Completed Portrait of Picasso," Stein sets up the expectation of a numerical series and then doesn't follow through:

> One.
> I land.
> Two.
> I land
> Three.
> The land.
> Three.
> The land.
> Three.
> The land.
> Two.
> I land.
> Two.
> I land.
> One.
> I land.
> Two.
> I land.[47]

One would expect four to follow three in this series. Instead Stein repeats *three* several times, *two* twice, *one* once, and then *two* again. Stein has also set up expectation of exact repetition of the phrase *I land*, but she shifts unexpectedly to another phrase that completely alters the meaning of the word *land* by using it as a noun rather than as a verb.

The items in a list are always linked by some principle of association, which is the basic operation of list-making. They have been chosen to be part of that list because they are related in some way. Items in a list are not combined in a formal syntactic structure; they are merely juxtaposed. A conventional sentence cannot be built from the items in a list because very often the words in the list may be all the same part of speech (very often nouns). If they are different parts of speech, they may appear in a hopelessly scrambled order that makes it impossible to read the list as a sentence. Thus propositions about a particular thing become impossible when *combination* is suppressed. Without syntax, the reader must come to terms with each item on the list as an entity with an unstated (though sometimes inferred) relationship to the other entities on that list. The reader must deal with each item on the list as something that is "simply different." In the lecture "Composition as Explanation," Stein says: "In this natural way of creating it then that it was simply different everything being alike it was simply different, this kept on leading one to lists. Lists naturally for a while and by lists I mean a series."[48] Steiner points out that in these lists, Stein was emphasizing the existence of objects as "things-in-themselves, self-contained and independent of human creation," and that "the lists themselves contained elements linked by parts of speech and parallelism within the progression of the series, but intransigently individual, unique, single."[49]

In spite of the elimination of sentences in many of Stein's works, structure often remains because a list is a way to logically organize and order items without relying on sentences. The list shares with the sentence the fact that its words can be serially ordered. But the order of the list is not necessarily mandatory or conventional, whereas word order in a sentence is largely dictated by grammar and is certainly not optional or even greatly variable if the sentence is to keep both its meaning and its status as a sentence.

Stein's emphatic and repeated use of the list and other asyntactical formats is a logical extension of the experiments with scrambled and truncated syntax that flowered in *Tender Buttons*. Perhaps by recourse to the list she was experimenting with communication without the sentence. When syntax is eliminated, verb tenses also disappear, along with time, as one focuses on each individual item without temporal or logical relationships to other items created by grammatical links. In "Composition as Explanation" Stein said: "The time of the composition . . . has been at times a present thing . . . a past thing . . . a future thing. . . . In my beginning it was a continuous present a beginning again and again and again and again, it was a series it was a list it was a similarity and everything different."[50]

The basic operation of list-making is association of selected items and so involves chiefly the vertical axis of language. However, the list can associate items in two different ways: by similarity and by contiguity. Items can be related by contiguity, that is, linked within a temporal or spatial context or, in Barthes's words, by an associative relation whose "terms are really united *in praesentia*."[51] For example, a list of all the foods one has eaten throughout a forty-eight-hour period or of all the items found in a certain drawer would link items contiguously in time or space. The items listed in the following passage from "Oval" are usually linked in time and space:

> Hems.
> Hem stitched.
> Sheet.
> Sheets.
> Hem stitched.
> Towels.
> Hem stitches.
> Soils.
> Soil towels.
> Hem stitched.
> Hem stitched.[52]

Towels and sheets are certainly found together in a linen closet or laundry basket. The hem (hemstitched, of course) is spatially linked to the sheet and the towel. And soil clings to the surface of the towel. This is a spatial association: soil and towels are not similar, but they are often found together.

Items not found together in time or space can be associated by similarity. For example, one might list all the foods containing vitamin A or all the unmarried female characters created by William Shakespeare. This type of association dominates in the following list created by Stein: "Martha: Carrots and Artichokes, marguerites and roses."[53] Although one might argue that contiguity links all four items at least potentially, since all items might be spatially linked in a garden, similarity dominates. Carrots and artichokes are vegetables; marguerites and roses both refer to flowers as well as to women's names. Roses and artichokes have a similar configuration, each having many petals. (Also, carrots and daisies are both rather pedestrian compared to the elegance of artichokes and roses.)

Although Stein sometimes constructs her lists on association by either similarity or contiguity, she sometimes combines the two principles. This is quite natural: an absolute split between the two operations would be artificial. But Stein's lists sometimes baffle the reader by breaking down logical categories and systemization. For example, even though association based on similarity dominates in the following excerpt, one can find association by spatial or temporal contiguity in the list.

MARYAS: Examples of wool.
  Samples of wool. Sheep and wool.
  Lions and wool.
  Lions and sheep and wool. Lions and sheep and wool
and silk.
  Silk and sheep and wool and silk. Silk and sheep, silk and wool,
silk and sheep and silk and wool and silk. Sheep and silk and wool
and silk and sheep.[54]

On the concrete level, lion and sheep are associated by similarity because they are both animals. They are also opposites in their metaphorical associations: power and ferocity versus vulnerability and gentleness:
The lion lies down with the lamb. This metaphorical relationship is
based on opposition, not similarity; but opposites can be chosen in an
operation of similarity. Jakobson points out that "selection and substitution are two faces of the same operation,"[55] and that "The two opposite tropes, metaphor and metonymy, present the most condensed
expression of two basic modes of relation: the internal relation of similarity (and contrast) underlies the metaphor; the external relation of
contiguity (and remoteness) determines the metonymy."[56] Many words
in the above passage from "A List" are also linked by both literal and
figurative similarity and contiguity. Silk and wool are literally similar
as fabrics used to make clothing, though their textures and weights are
opposite. Silk is smooth and light; wool is rough and heavy. But the
association of sheep and wool is based on associations of signifiers (the
words themselves), such as rhyme—example/sample—and the repetition of sounds (alliterated and single). It even seems that the word *wolf*
is being evoked through its similarity to *wool* and its associations with
clothing and *sheep* in the phrase *a wolf in sheep's clothing*.

The basic operation of list-making is selection and association of
items, but unless a list is totally amorphous and random, the operation
of combination operates in ordering the items. Even though there may
be no syntax in it and even though it may be impossible to combine the
words into a sentence, a list may have a different, nonsyntactical order.
Combination (the relationship of items *in praesentia*) determines the
order of items on a list, and that order may be either rational or random.

Lists may be ordered alphabetically. This is the basic structure of "To
Do: Alphabets and Birthdays" discussed earlier, in which characters
and actions are invented to use each letter of the alphabet in order.
Alphabetical order is an arbitrary rather than dramatic structure for the
events of each narrative. For example, one narrative concerns Zed, a
little girl who wants a zebra for her birthday.[57] Butor points out that

alphabetical order can be a catalyst for dramatic action: "if alphabetical
order is not based on objective relations between the things designated
by the words, it can nevertheless determine relations between them; we
all remember the role our position in the alphabetical list played for us
among our classmates in school."[58]

Another rational principle Stein used to order a list is chronology.
This is the underlying structure of "Birthdays: A Birthday Book":

> September the twenty-second thirty days has September.
>
> September the twenty-third April June.
>
> September the twenty-fourth and November.
>
> September the twenty-fifth all the others.
>
> September the twenty-sixth thirty-one.
>
> September the twenty-seventh except the second.
>
> September the twenty-eighth the second.
>
> September the twenty-ninth month alone.
>
> September the thirtieth but a year.
>
> September a year gives it twenty-nine.[59]

Stein plays with the "Thirty Days Hath September" jingle, which links
months not by chronological order or contiguity but by similarity of the
number of days each contains. Yet the overriding order of this list and
of the work as a whole is a chronological and numerical order that
structures "A Birthday Book" day by day, month by month.

Here is another example of the chronologically ordered list, from
Stein's "History or Messages from History," written in 1930:

Flowers	7	And lovely flowers mostly roses pansies and dahlias.
Herbs	7.15	And very delicate and spicy herbs.
Francis	7.30	He was quite welcome was he not.
Hat	8	A hat very well suited to the usage for which it was and is intended.
Beans	9.30	A great many beans.
Basket	10.30	He is sometimes a trial of patience.
Bathe	11.30	A pleasure and a refreshment.[60]

The passage seems to be a chronological list of activities correlated
with the times indicated in the second column. The third column gives

short comments on the activity or event, which may help to identify it. (Perhaps this passage draws on Stein's life at Belignin, where there were gardens of flowers and vegetables.) The activities referred to might be picking flowers and herbs, receiving a visitor (taking his hat), picking (or shelling or stringing) beans, tending to Basket (her dog), and taking a bath.

Both of the above examples are lists organized not merely on one ordering principle but on two. Again Stein toys with the reader's expectation of rational structures. She either makes the structure so complex that it is hard to perceive or else raises such expectations only to leave them completely unfulfilled. But why does Stein abandon the sentence for the list, and why do her lists seem to lack a coherent principle of ordering? This is the same person, after all, whose desire for order led her to undertake the classification of all human beings into types.

Perhaps the seemingly random, orderless, and arational word heap apparent in Stein's use of the list in her plays and elsewhere presents a different model for looking at life. Weinstein implies that words heaped together can portray the simultaneity of human experience. A new desire to avoid imposing order on the world may be why Stein so often puts only enough order into her lists so that they cannot be dismissed as totally random. This is a frustrating tease for the reader or critic looking for order because it is even difficult to decide whether the list is random or structured. Through writing *Tender Buttons*, Stein came to place more value on the immediate perception of the world than on the effort to classify and order experience, as in *The Making of Americans*. Perhaps this is why Stein not only plays with, but often subverts, principles of association and order that normally function in list-making. Readers' expectations that such rational principles underlie the list are constantly raised as they hunt for some kind of order; then hopes are dashed by Stein's inconsistency in following that order through. The reader is often finally forced to take each word on its own terms, in isolation. William Gass said of her writing, "[E]ach word is an object to Gertrude Stein, something in a list, like the roll call of the ships, and lists are delightful simply for the words that are on them."[61]

The sentence, the basis of prose, has been eliminated. The noun and, by implication, poetry and the act of selection have won. But although Stein's use of the list continued throughout her career, prose reappeared in the thirties and was eventually combined with aspects of her poetic style to create a new style that crosses traditional boundaries between the genres and even her own definitions of prose and poetry.

CHAPTER FOUR

CLARITY RETURNS:

"IDA" AND "THE GEOGRAPHICAL HISTORY

OF AMERICA"

AROUND THE 1930s Stein approached intelligibility again by combining elements of both obscure styles and allowing both selection and combination to become fully operative again.[1] In works such as *Ida* and *The Geographical History of America*, language is both discursive and arbitrary, and the boundaries between poetry and prose blur, a tendency that Steiner noticed in Stein's work of this period in general.[2] Stein's writing does not return to clarity unchanged. From the influence of cubist painters, she retains a playful awareness of the artist's power to produce a nonmimetic work that exists on its own terms rather than as a representation of the world as it is.

The publication of *The Autobiography of Alice B. Toklas* in 1933[3] marks not only an important milestone in Stein's literary fortunes, but also the flowering of a new trend in her stylistic development. Bridgman says of that work's composition, "After twenty years of enigmatic utterances, Gertrude Stein at last chose to speak in a voice of singular clarity. She was fifty-eight years old."[4] Relative clarity emerges in much of Stein's writing of the thirties, most notably with the *Autobiography* written in 1932.[5] This trend appears in her theoretical writings and lectures, *Lectures in America* (1934); *What Are Masterpieces and Why Are There So Few of Them* (1935); her so-called philosophical meditations, such as *The Geographical History of America; or, The Relation of Human Nature to the Human Mind* (1935); her writing about herself, *Everybody's Autobiography* (1936), *Wars I Have Seen* (1942), and about *Picasso* (1938). But even more significantly, this new impulse toward clarity is seen even in some of her creative work, such as *Ida: A Novel* (1940), *The World Is Round* (1938), and *Mrs. Reynolds: A Novel* (1940). Bridgman proposes biographical explanations for the appearance of this clearly written work; among them are "heightened fame, a creative slump, and the hope of pleasing Alice."[6] He even raises the question of whether Toklas had a hand in writing the book. Bridgman said of the *Autobiography*:

> Its ironic precision was utterly foreign to Gertrude Stein, and therefore it is natural to wonder if her companion was in any way responsible for the drastic stylistic metamorphosis.
>
> One possiblity is sufficiently heretical that no one has dared advance it directly; but there have been hints that Alice Toklas composed her own autobiography.[7]

But one need not speculate so broadly about Stein's new clarity. It is more fruitful to examine her stylistic escape from deepest obscurity as she allows both axes of language to become fully operative again.

Up to this point Stein's obscurity had been manifested in several styles. First there was the earliest obscure style of her pre-1912 portraits and of the latter portions of *The Making of Americans*, which emphasized syntax and suppressed vocabulary: "He was knowing some who were being ones at the end of the beginning of being living when he was at the end of the beginning being living. In a way he was one with them, in many ways he was not one with them. He was one with them in being one being one of them, in being one completely understanding something." (*The Making of Americans*, p. 874.) Then there was the second obscure style, represented by *Tender Buttons* as well as by the poems and portraits written after 1912, which extended vocabulary and suppressed syntax:

APPLE

Apple plum, carpet steak, seed clam, colored wine, calm seen, cold cream, best shake, potato, potato and no no gold work with pet, a green seen is called bake and change sweet is bready, a little piece a little piece please.

A little piece please. Cane again to the presupposed and ready eucalyptus tree, count out sherry and ripe plates and little corners of a kind of ham. This is use. [*Tender Buttons*, p. 48.]

Another extreme outgrowth of this second kind of obscurity is the lists
and a vertical format, as syntax, sentences, and paragraphs are all eliminated as in "Study Nature" (1918):

> I do.
> Victim.
> Sales
> Met
> Wipe
> Her
> Less.[8]

This phenomenon began about the same time as the *Tender Buttons*
style in 1912. This style, in some ways an extension of the second
obscurity that Stein classified as poetry, often occurs in combination
with paragraphs, as poetry is expressed in both vertical and horizontal
formats. But in both cases, the operation of selection (vertical axis) is
stressed. Up to this point none of these obscure styles or variations of
styles had been *conventionally* comprehensible. Only when syntax and
vocabulary, selection and combination are simultaneously allowed to
come within a normal range of development does Stein's writing begin
to "make sense," as in the following passage from *Ida* (1940): "It was
a nice time then. Instead of working or having his money Arthur just
listened to anybody. It made him sleepy and he was never more than
half awake and in his sleep he had a way of talking about sugar and
cooking. He also used to talk about medicine glasses."[9] Although the
events described seem fantastic, the passage is certainly understandable. In *The Geographical History of America* (p. 199), Stein incorporates similar poetic passages expressed both in paragraphs and in columns:

> And human nature is what everybody knows and time and iden-
> tity is what everybody knows and they are not master-pieces and
> yet everybody knows that master-pieces say what they do say about
> human nature and time and identity, and what is the use, there is
> no abuse in what is the use, there is no use. Why not.
> Now listen. What is conversation.
> Conversation is only interesting if nobody hears.
> Hear hear.
> Masterpieces are second to none.
> One and one.

Although both of these passages are a bit eccentric and the second is a
bit hard to read because punctuation is lacking, they are certainly clearer

than much of Stein's writing since the relatively conventional prose narratives in *Three Lives* (1905–6).

Although some critics, who consider Stein's early conventional prose (*Three Lives*, *Things as They Are*) her best writing, see her obscurity as a loss, her later return to intelligibility in the thirties does not imply that her work evolved toward this as a goal or that her later work is better or more interesting than *The Making of Americans* or *Tender Buttons* because it is clearer. In fact, her more obscure work is more innovative, and on that account it is more interesting and more important. Much of her later work merely repeats or modifies the earlier stylistic innovations.

This reemerging clarity may have been just a response to Stein's relatively late awareness of audience, which began to grow during the early thirties,[10] and a new desire to make herself clear to that audience. In fact, this awareness of audience raised questions of identity that became key concerns in both *Ida* and the *Geographical History*. Brinnin writes that "Identity, in particular the identity of genius, was the main subject" of *The Geographical History of America*.[11] The theme of identity and audience comes up often in passages like the following (pp. 112–13): "I am I because my little dog knows me[12] . . . and yet the little dog knowing me does not really make me be I no not really because after all being I I am I has really nothing to do with the little dog knowing me, he is my audience, but an audience never does prove to you that you are you." Brinnin also points out that in *Ida*, Stein tried to examine and resolve "the problem of identity that had obsessed her ever since she had become famous,"[13] and which was partially responsible for a creative slump. In *Everybody's Autobiography* Stein discusses this problem, which she experienced after *The Autobiography of Alice B. Toklas* was published: "All this time I did no writing. I had written and was writing nothing. Nothing inside me needed to be written. . . . And I was not writing. I began to worry about identity. I had always been I because I had words that had to be written inside me. . . . I am I because my little dog knows me. But was I I when I had no written word inside me."[14]

The fact that Stein's writing becomes more comprehensible does not mean that she renounced her earlier obscurities. In fact, she incorporated elements of both of her obscure styles into the works that followed. The resulting increase in clarity is no more than one would expect, given Jakobson's observation that suppression of either combination or selection causes serious disintegration in the comprehensibility of language. A look at the novel *Ida* and *The Geographical History of America*, a nonfiction philosophical meditation, shows how Stein combines elements of her first obscure style, which emphasized the horizontal axis of language, with elements of her second obscure style, which emphasized the vertical axis.

In "And Now," printed in *Vanity Fair* in 1934 during her U.S. tour, Stein said, "I write the way I used to write in *The Making of Americans*."[15] This is not strictly true. In these later works she no longer restricts vocabulary or emphasizes the present participle as in *The Making of Americans*. Although she had been producing works emphasizing the vertical format and the list for some time and continued to do so until her death, the paragraph reappears more frequently during the 1930s. And although one can still occasionally find fragments and fused sentences in these works, the predominant syntax approaches a normal range, as in at least some of her writing she turned away from the almost exclusive use of isolated words and phrases. But the use of the sentence and paragraph is not the sole basis for distinguishing prose from poetry in Stein's work. *Tender Buttons* is written in paragraphs and looks like conventional prose, but Stein classifies it as poetry because of its emphasis on the word. Even though written in paragraphs, other works, such as "The Portrait of Mabel Dodge" (1912) and *Lucy Church Amiably* (1927), would be classified as poetry according to Stein's criteria.

In the reemerging clarity of her later works, not only does syntax approach (but not reach) orthodoxy, but sentence length is more conventional than either the long sentences of *The Making of Americans* or the short phrases of *Tender Buttons* and works written in columns. Here is an example taken from *The Geographical History of America* (p. 80):

> Are there any customs and habits in America there is geography and what what is the human mind. The human mind is there because they write and they do not forget or remember and they do not go away and come back again. That is what the human mind does not human nature but the human mind. Listen to the human-mind.
>
> I will tell a story about the human mind what is the story.
>
> It is the story of Bennett.
>
> Bennett has an uncle who is as young as he is that is to say he is about the same age and age has nothing to do with the human-mind.
>
> When a great many hear you that is an audience and if a great many hear you what difference does it make.
>
> Bennett and his uncle do not know anything about that.

And why not. Because that has nothing to do with the human mind.

Although there are a few run-on sentences in the above passage, most sentences are correctly constructed in terms of grammar, although the lack of punctuation makes them hard to follow (as in *The Making of Americans*). Here, most individual sentences are understandable, despite vague pronoun references in the first paragraph (another vestige of the first obscure style). Most of the difficulty in the passage comes from Stein's digressions and from the separations of several lines between related statements about a particular topic.

As in much of Stein's writing of the thirties and forties, this passage has more semantic meaning than works of the *Tender Buttons* style. The syntax is more conventional and also has more specific content than the "abstract" style of the late *The Making of Americans* and the early portraits, and the vocabulary is not so stringently restricted and limited to general words:

> One day it was not Tuesday, two people came to see her great-aunt. They came in very carefully. They did not come in together. First one came and then the other one. One of them had some orange blossoms in her hand. That made Ida feel funny. Who were they? She did not know. . . . A third one came along, this one was a man and he had orange blossoms in his hat brim. He took off his hat and said to himself here I am, I wish to speak to myself. Here I am. Then he went on in the house. [*Ida*, p. 9.]

Stein's statements are sometimes disconcerting, but they do make sense. The subject and verb are no longer semantically disjunctive as in *Tender Buttons*. The passage also conveys enough concrete information to communicate an idea. In *Ida* Stein combines elements of both earlier styles, producing comprehensible writing, at least on the level of the individual sentence.

However, one can also see traces of the kind of obscurity found in *The Making of Americans*. Although the characters in *Ida* are given names rather than just pronouns (as in the extremes of Stein's first obscure style), *Ida* resembles that style in presenting only very general information about the characters' external qualities. Most characters are identified only by first names, and "biographical" information is most superficial. For example, one of Ida's many husbands is introduced to the reader as follows (p. 35):

> Ida married Frank Arthur.
> Arthur had been born right in the middle of a big country.

He knew when he was a tiny boy that the earth was round so it never was a surprise to him. He knew that trees had green leaves and that there was snow when time for snow came and rain when time for rain came. He knew a lot.

Action in *Ida* may also be presented very generally, even though there are more verbs expressing action than in the early portraits or the end of *The Making of Americans*. The reader is not given a detailed description that shows the action, but merely a generalized summary of the event (p. 77):

And so Ida was in Washington.
One day, it happened again and again some one said something to her, they said Oh Ida, did you see me. Oh yes she said. Ida never did not see anybody, she always saw everybody and said she saw them. She made no changes about seeing them.
So he said to her Ida, your name is Ida isn't it, yes she said, and he said I thought your name was Ida, I thought you were Ida and I thought your name is Ida.
It is, she said.
They sat down.

This passage presents only a general picture of the event. Its location is no more specific than Washington. Where did they sit down? Ida's interlocutor is not identified by gender in the first paragraph but is referred to only as someone, although *he* is used in the next paragraph. (His name is eventually supplied on that page, however.) Other general words, such as *something, anybody, everybody*, and *them*, are reminiscent of *The Making of Americans*, as is the repetition.

Ida is also abstract in another sense, in the same sense that *Tender Buttons* is abstract. Although the vocabulary of *Ida* is more concrete than that of *The Making of Americans*, the work as a whole resembles *Tender Buttons*—not in syntax or semantic content, both of which are much more orthodox—but in its freedom from fidelity to the external world as referent. Although Stein has returned to prose, the discoveries made while writing the "poetry" of *Tender Buttons* have had their influence. The prose of *The Making of Americans* and similar works was tied to representation of the referent (capturing a person's basic nature, creating a history of all human possibilities), however generalized and eccentric that representation was. But now, in this new kind of prose, language is used arbitrarily, not only in fiction, but also in Stein's critical, philosophical, and autobiographical writing.

While much of the language in this new prose conveys information and discursive thought, Stein also includes in it elements of her "poetic" style. In the second lecture of *Narration*, she said:

> In the beginning there really was no difference between poetry and prose. . . . How could there be . . . since the name of anything was then as important as anything . . . that could be said about anything. . . .
>
> [T]he Old Testament did this thing there was not really any difference between prose and poetry then. . . . [16]
>
> Well and now, now that we have been realizing that anything having a beginning and middle and ending is not what is making anything anything, and now that everything is so completely moving in the name of anything is not really anything to interest any one about anything, now it is coming that once again nobody can be certain that narrative is existing that prose and poetry have different meanings. [17]

Once Stein discovered "poetry" while writing *Tender Buttons*, she did not separate it from the rest of her work. Many of her plays contain some poetry, and it also crops up in her prose works, both fiction and nonfiction. For one thing, many of her prose works contain what Copeland calls Stein's "treatment of language as if it were an autotelic rather than a representational entity." [18] That is, Stein pays attention to the word itself and to its qualities as a signifier, which is what she considered the essence of poetry to be in *Tender Buttons* and similar works. *Ida: A Novel* is often interrupted by passages just as poetic, by Stein's definition, as anything in *Tender Buttons* or in Stein's long poem "Before the Flowers of Friendship Faded Friendship Faded." One way in which poetry manifests itself in *Ida* is in whimsical wordplay. Among its many puns is, for example, Ida's dog named Love, who was born blind, a pun on an old cliché (p. 10). Ida tells this dog, "Later on they will call me a suicide blonde because my twin will have dyed her hair" (p. 11), another pun.

Stein also uses rhyme within her prose. Sometimes the essentially linear, though often discontinuous, narrative line is interrupted by passages of rhyme that may be only one line long. Stein's rhyme often functions as a closural device at the end of a discursive statement or paragraph: "Anybody likes to know about then and now, Ida was one and it is easy to have one sister and be a twin too and be a triplet three and be a quartet and four and be a quintuplet it is easy to have four but that just about does shut the door" (*Ida*, p. 42). Not only rhyme, but wordplay also is characteristic of the poetic *Tender Buttons* style. Besides the jingle at the end of the above passage, there is also a pun on the word *too*. *Quartet* is substituted for the similar word *quadruplet*. Thus Stein plays games with the reader's expectations and demands attention to words qua words.

Stein occasionally even interrupts the prose narrative of *Ida* with a little poem arranged vertically (p. 116).

> For a four.
> She shut the door.
> They dropped in.
> And drank gin.
> I'd like a conversation with Ida.

Here vestiges of the poetic style include not only rhyme but also truncation of the sentence into fragments. Sometimes poetic digressions are much longer. Whole paragraphs bounce along in sing-song rhythm, with several rhymes within the line. The following passage (pp. 122–23) is probably the longest poetic digression in *Ida*:

> Listen to me I, I am a spider, you must not mistake me for the sky, the sky red at night is a sailor's delight, the sky red in the morning is a sailor's warning, you must not mistake me for the sky, I am I, I am a spider and in the morning any morning I bring sadness and mourning and at night if they see me at night I bring them delight, do not mistake me for the sky, not I, do not mistake me for a dog who howls at night and causes no delight, a dog says the bright moonlight makes him go mad with desire to bring sorrow to any one sorrow and sadness, the dog says the night the bright moonlight brings madness and grief, but says the spider I, I am a spider, a big spider or a little spider, it is all alike, a spider green or gray, there is nothing else to say, I am a spider and I know and I always tell everybody so, to see me at night brings them delight, to see me in the morning brings mourning, and if you see me at night, and I am a sight, because I am dead having died up by night, even so dead at night I still cause delight, I dead bring delight to anyone who sees me at night, and so every one can see me sleep tight who has seen me at night.

Here characteristics of *The Making of Americans* and *Tender Buttons* are combined. As in *The Making of Americans*, Stein has created a paragraph-length sentence, sometimes linked by conjunctions and sometimes by clauses run together. The repetition is also characteristic of the earlier prose style. "I am a spider" is repeated four times; "you must not mistake me for the sky" is repeated three times, and so forth. However, the participles and genderless pronouns have been dropped, making the work easier to understand.

But although the syntax of the quoted sentence is stretched unmercifully, characteristics of Stein's poetic style dominate. Rhyme and rhythm are used here more than in *Tender Buttons*. The quality of the word, rather than its semantic content, predominates. Many phrases are apparently generated for the sake of the rhythm and/or rhyme. Many more adjectives and nouns appear here than in Stein's first obscure style. The words *spider* and *mourning* are associated, evoking the idea of a black widow spider through the association of *mourning* and *widow*. These associations all function along the vertical axis of language and are based on similarity. (In fact, the subject of the entire passage is superstition, the positing of a causal relationship based on the observation of similar patterns of events.)

Although much of the language in *Ida* functions to carry the narrative forward, some of the language (both in the digressions and the narrative) is used plastically as in the *Tender Buttons* style. Yet this use of language is juxtaposed with language that moves toward abstraction in much the same way as did *The Making of Americans*, as in the passage discussed above (ch. 1, pp. 9–10).

However, despite the lyrical passages, *Ida* is predominately a return to prose and, in some ways, a return to the traditions of prose fiction. In her transatlantic interview with Robert Bartlett Haas, Stein said that after she wrote *Four Saints in Three Acts* in 1932, she "went back to the form of narration."[19] In *Ida*, once again a central character is followed throughout the narrative as in the earlier stories of *Three Lives*, "Melanctha," "The Good Anna," and "The Gentle Lena." But Stein's return to the prose narrative has been greatly influenced by the discovery made in the course of writing *Tender Buttons* that language can be used arbitrarily. In *Ida* Stein extends the artist's arbitrary power over language to the very structure of the narrative. The action in *Ida* is not only episodic and temporally noncontiguous, as in *The Making of Americans*; it is also alogical. As a story *Ida* makes no sense in causal terms. The logic is the logic of the fantasy. *Ida* makes the kind of sense *Alice in Wonderland* does.

Although the novel tells a story, the plot seems to be what Copeland would call self-generative. For example, many characters are apparently introduced only because they bear the names of U.S. presidents, e.g., Andrew, Abraham, and George. The narrative grows out of the language and is very often subordinated to it, rather than vice versa. The logic of *Ida* arbitrarily suspends laws of causality and chronology; Ida's description of her dog Polybe (p. 103), for example, seems almost as fantastic as Lewis Carroll's description of the Cheshire cat:

Polybe was not a small dog he was a hound and he had stripes red and black like only a zebra's stripes are white and black but Polybe's stripes were as regular as that and his front legs were long, all his family could kill a rabbit with a blow of their front paw, that is really why they danced in the moonlight, they thought they were chasing rabbits, any shadow was a rabbit to them and there are lots of shadows on a hillside in the summer under a bright moon.

Events don't develop as logical consequences of other events, but occur suddenly and arbitrarily, with no motive or explanation supplied: "Ida was married again this time he came from Boston, she remembered his name. She was good friends with all her husbands" (p. 62); or: "Ida never saw Arthur again. She just did not" (p. 40).

The constraints of temporal contiguity are often rejected along with assumptions of logic and causality in prose, assumptions that are basically diachronic and associated with the horizontal axis of language:

Narrative has been the telling of anything because there has been always a feeling that something followed another thing that there was succession in happening. . . . What has made the Old Testament such permanently good reading is that . . . in the Old Testament writing there really was not . . . any succession of anything. . . . In the Old Testament writing there is really no actual conclusion that anything is progressing that one thing is succeeding happening is a narrative of anything . . . but most writing has been a real narrative writing a telling of the story of anything in the way that the thing has been happening and now everything is not that thing there is at present not a sense of anything being successively happening, moving is in every direction beginning and ending is not really exciting . . . and this has come to be a natural thing in a perfectly natural way that the narrative of today is not a narrative of succession as all the writing for a good many hundreds of years has been.[20]

Stein doubted the interest of traditional narrative for modern readers, who see and hear of so many events in the media, yet see little action in their own lives. Stein's observation that modern Americans spend most of their time standing around doing nothing is reflected in *Ida*. The protagonist spends a lot of time just resting. "Ida led a very easy life, that is she got up and sat up and went in and came out and rested and went to bed" (p. 68). This deemphasis of action obviously makes the time of the adventure irrelevant to the order of the novel. When the action presented is undramatic, mundane, or inconsequential, chronology becomes irrelevant. Quotidian events are by definition repeated actions. In *Ida* Stein shows the irrelevance of chronological time to an inconsequential life:

> One day did not come after another day to Ida. Ida never took on yesterday or tomorrow, she did not take on months either nor did she take on years. Why should she when she had always been the same, what ever happened there she was . . . resting and everything happening. Sometimes something did happen, she knew to whom she had been married but that was not anything happening, she knew about clothes and resting but that was not anything happening. [*Ida*, p. 135.]

As action is suppressed in favor of mental processes, the mental time of perception displaces chronological order in Stein's writing. Despite the roughly chronological order of events, time in *Ida* has less to do with chronological or diachronic (horizontal) time than with mythological or synchronic (vertical) time. Sutherland sees *Ida* as a legend and a myth; Ida's activities are recounted out of time: "In a vague way, *Ida* is about the Duchess of Windsor, but it is really the story of what Gertrude Stein called a 'publicity saint,' that is a person who neither does anything nor is connected with anything but who by sheer force of existence in being there holds the public attention and becomes a legend."[21] Events occur for no reason and out of time, as in the presentation of one of Ida's marriages (p. 75 above). As in myth the particulars are less important than the essential structure of the event. Sutherland classifies many of Stein's late works, such as *Ida* (1940), *Picasso* (1938), *Brewsie and Willie* (1945), as legends.[22] Stein, always faithful to present tense, could deal with the past by making it into a legend, which is eternally present. The legend solves the problem of time in the narrative, as Sutherland implies:

> Narrative cannot possibly go on living by its truth to the historical facts or to the psychological or moral facts, or by having one thing lead to another; it now has to go on the conviction that sheer happening in the immediate present, and above all in the immediate written present, is the final reality. In short the business of the narrative artist is now . . . the creation of legend.[23]

Stein also tries to conquer the traditionally chronological and linear organization of the novel. She uses associative time, as events narrated evoke similar events associated with it in the narrator's mind, though there may be no chronological connection. For example, *Ida* contains a very long digression (pp. 96–106), absolutely extraneous to the action, in which the protagonist catalogs and comments on all the dogs she has ever owned. The only apparent reason for the sudden appearance of this digression is that the subject happened to come to Ida or to Stein's mind: "So Ida was left alone, and she began to sit again. And sitting she thought about her life with dogs and this was it" (p. 96). Within the six-page digression that follows this passage, the movement of thought is largely associative. Although Ida at first seems to describe her dogs in the chronological order in which she owned them, she soon digresses and makes links on the basis of similarities: "That was all. Then there were a lot of dogs but none of them interesting. Then there was a little dog, a black and tan and he hung himself on a string when somebody left him. He had not been so interesting, but the way he died made him very interesting" (p. 97).

Stein used this digressive associative time in *The Making of Americans*, but her use of it in *Ida* is different in two ways. First, the digressions in *The Making of Americans* are still prose and of the same style as the narrative that is being interrupted, while in *Ida* they are very often poetic by Stein's criteria. Secondly, in *The Making of Americans* Stein conveyed a sense of the duration of both external and internal processes (partially through the participle as well as through long, tortuous sentences). Both her early portraits and *Tender Buttons* are static and timeless because they have no narrative per se. But in *Ida* Stein tries to tell a story without creating a sense of duration. The passage of time is announced but is not shown or described for the reader, as in the following account of Ida's childhood (p. 14):

> Ida gradually was a little older and every time she was a little older some one else took care of her. She liked the change of address because in that way she never had to remember what her address was and she did not like having to remember. It was so easy to forget the last address and soon she really forgot to guess what the next address was.
>
> Little by little she knew how to read and write and really she said and she was right it was not necessary for her to know anything else. And so quite gradually little by little she grew older.

We aren't shown Ida's development over time, but are merely told that she "was gradually a little older," "gradually little by little she grew older," and learned to read and write "little by little." The gradual passage of time is just announced. This is certainly not a detailed description that captures a feeling of duration. But it does convey the transience and probably loneliness of Ida's upbringing (she can't remember her last address), as well as the shallowness of her education ("it was not necessary for her to know anything else").[24] Evident here is Stein's desire to capture the essence of a person or action without directly describing either.

Representing the chronology of passing time during an event does not concern Stein. She does not care about the order or duration of Ida's adventures. Instead she represents the duration and order of the narrator's subjective mental time. In this novel the time of the telling is more important than the time of the vague, episodic action. Although Stein was interested in this kind of time throughout her career, the portrayal of the circuitous workings of mental time is not her invention. It is at least as old as *Tristram Shandy*, but as new as Robbe-Grillet's *Project for a Revolution in New York*.

Stein's *The Geographical History of America; or, The Relation of Human Nature to the Human Mind* and similar nonfiction works also combine goals and elements of Stein's prose and poetic styles. *The Geographical History of America*, a kind of philosophical meditation, is more sober than *Ida*. One goal of the work is ostensibly to explore simple ideas with some degree of clarity. On the very first page, Stein announces: "These are ordinary ideas. If you please these are ordinary ideas" (p. 53). Much of what she writes here can be classified as discursive, expository prose. The following passage is a straight-forward and clear observation. "I used to wonder when I saw boys who had just been boys and they went into an office to work and they came out with a handful of papers and I said to them how since you never had anything to do with papers before these business papers were given to you how do you know what to do with them. They just did. They knew what to do with them" (p. 133). Although sometimes vague and hard to follow, this book is still relatively clear because its vocabulary and syntax both approach normal usage. Yet one finds traces of both obscure styles in this work.

Many observations about the style of *Ida* are also true of *The Geographical History of America*. The work contains some very long sentences, some as long as an average paragraph. Their construction is much like that of the long sentences in *The Making of Americans*. But, as in *Ida*, the participles are gone and the vocabulary is less radically limited. The syntax of the following sentence-paragraph resembles that of *The Making of Americans*:

> I know so well the relation of a simple center and a continuous design to the land as one looks down on it, a wandering line as

one looks down on it, a quarter section as one looks down on it,
the shadows of each tree on the snow and the woods on each side
and the land higher up between it and I know so well how in spite
of the fact that the human mind has not looked at it the human
mind has it to know that it is there like that, notwithstanding that
the human mind has liked what it has which has not been like that.
[*The Geographical History of America*, p. 85].

This sentence is roughly one hundred words long and contains at least
nine clauses. There is some repetition resembling both the style of *The
Making of Americans* and the repetition of rhythmic phrases ("as one
looks down on it") with words arbitrarily inserted as in *Tender Buttons*.
The syntax is definitely that of *The Making of Americans*. On the whole,
the vocabulary is still relatively small and simple. Some key terms,
e.g., *human mind*, *human nature*, and *identity*, are repeated. Although
mainly discursive, this prose work is also often interrupted by snatches
of Stein's poetry, wordplay, passages that bounce along in singsong
rhythm and rhyme within the line, and the occasional use of vertical
structures. Alongside the extended sentences in *The Geographical History of America* are many fragments in passages that emphasize the
vertical axis of language.

When a "play" is introduced into *The Geographical History of America*, as in the following passage (p. 161), one can see Stein's use of
fragments, puns, vertical format, and other devices characteristic of her
second "poetic" style.

Part I

I am not confused in mind because I have a human
mind.

Part II

Yes which is.

Part I

Romance and money one by one.

Part II

Lolo.

Part II

Care fully for me.
As often as carefully.
Each one of these words has to do with nothing that is
not romance and money.

Part III

Romance has nothing to do with human nature.

Part III
Neither has money.

Despite the truncated sentences and wordplay, some of her statements are perfectly orthodox declarative propositions, such as the next to last sentence above, "Romance has nothing to do with human nature." Such statements are also interspersed with labels (Part II) that parody the conventional linear division of a book into chapters and parts. As in *Ida*, *The Geographical History of America* challenges the linear organization of the book by playing with the order of chapters, as on page 141 where chapter 91 immediately precedes chapter 2. Stein also comments: "There is no reason why chapters should succeed each other since nothing succeeds another, not now any more. In the old novels yes but not now any more" (p. 90); and she announces, "I could have begun with Chapter I but anybody even I have had enough of that" (p. 95).

The obscurity that remains in the grammatically orthodox sentences of *The Geographical History of America* comes partly from failure to define or describe terms adequately, as in the following passage (p. 53): "Now the relationship of human nature to the human mind is this. / Human nature does not know this. / Human nature cannot know this." The next few lines clarify, but at this point the reader is already confused:

> What is it that human nature does not know. Human nature does not know that if every one did not die there would be no room for those who live now.
> Human nature can not know this.
> Now the relationship of human nature to the human mind is this.
> Human nature cannot know this.
> But the human mind can. It can know this.

Although one can follow the above passages, Stein is still leaping suddenly from one proposition to another without any intermediate steps, rather than following a sequence of logical development. In *The Geographical History of America*, she still uses pronouns without clearly designated antecedents, as she did in *The Making of Americans*. In the above passage, *this* refers to both what human nature can know and the relationship of human nature to the human mind, and that pronoun is used for three lines before any antecedent is mentioned at all.

Stein's philosophical musings are juxtaposed with internal rhymes that occur frequently enough to create the impression of a jingle. Passages similar to the following (p. 54) occur throughout the work: "After all would do we like to live to have lived, then if we do then everybody else has had to die and we have to cry because we too one day will have to die otherwise the others who will like to live could not come by." Stein also occasionally indulges in wordplay characteristic of *Tender Buttons*: "Money is interesting and romanticism not human nature and sadism. Make it another thing if you like sad is and sadism" (*The Geographical History of America*, p. 189). Some passages evoke a series of colorful images that Stein might classify as poetic:

> Tears of pleasure numbers have such pretty names. They have something to do with money and with trees and flat land, not with mountains or lakes, yes with blades of grass, not much a little but not much with flowers, some with birds not much with dogs . . . .
> They have nothing to do with dogs and human nature but have they anything to do with the human mind, they ought to have something to do with the human mind because they are so pretty and they can bring forth tears of pleasure [p. 115].

Discursive passages that emphasize the words as *signifieds* are juxtaposed with and interrupted by passages that emphasize poetic concerns, that is, the words as signifiers. In the latter the concern is with language as an entity in its own right, free to be used arbitrarily, not only as a carrier of meaning. And in the above passage, one can see language used both discursively and poetically.

In this combination of Stein's two obscure and most extreme styles, the distinctions blur between prose and poetry, lyricism and narrative, prosody and philosophy. In Thornton Wilder's introduction to *The Geographical History of America*, he says:

> Metaphysics is difficult enough; metaphysics by an artist is still more difficult; but metaphysics by an artist in a mood of gaity is most difficult of all. The subject matter of this book is grave, indeed. . . . But Miss Stein has always placed much emphasis on the spirit of play in an artist's work. The reward of difficult thinking is an inner exhilaration. Here is delight in words and in the virtuosity of using them exactly: Here is wit; here is mockery at the predecessors who approached these matters with so cumbrous a solemnity.[25]

The heaviness of philosophical prose is countered by the light and playful spirit and the "delight in words." The combination of poet and metaphysician is not altogether unheard of, as Wilder points out. "When the metaphysician is combined with the poet we get such unusual modes of expression as the myths of Plato, the prophetic books of Blake, and the difficult highly figured phrases in Keats' letters."[26]

In works like *Ida* and *The Geographical History of America*, which resist categorization as either prose or poetry, Stein seems to deny the clear separation of these two genres as self-contained and inviolate. Wendell Wilcox, in "A Note on Stein and Abstractionism," noted the blurring of Stein's own distinctions between prose and poetry and observed that in

> much of her prose you meet recurrence to and calling and re-calling upon a single person or thing, and the prose style which she invented for her use, being patterned and rhythmic not in the sense of set patterns and meters, but in the sense of the play and movement between the words themselves, has in it tone and a quality which comes close to poetry.
>
> Whitman years before had brought poetry as close to the boundary line of prose as poetry could come without becoming prose. In Stein we find that prose has been brought across the line which he left, and I rather think that in her own mind the distinction was lost, or to speak more accurately, abandoned.[27]

In both *Ida* and *The Geographical History of America*, Stein combines prose with poetry, and she returns to the temporal discontinuity of *The Making of Americans*. She is again interested in mental time, the time of telling, with its repetitions and digressions. But in these later works, digressions are likely to be poetic or even dramatic rather than just discursive prose. So use of the vertical axis of language found in Stein's second obscure style and developed further in the vertical format of her plays is combined with the essentially horizontal orientation of prose. This suggests that associative structures, the basis of poetry (those vertical systems of selection or sets of words associated in absentia by similarity), operate beneath the surface of the ongoing discursive chain of speech or stream of thought (a horizontal structure linking words *in praesentia* through combination). However logical the chain of speech, those associative structures—more or less conscious, more or less rational—are always there. By letting them surface and interrupt the linear flow of her narrative or discursive writing, Stein represents the thought process, which is in reality similarly interrupted, even though most authors censor such digressions and diversions before thought becomes speech or writing.

One can see, then, why it is so disconcerting to have a nonfiction prose work such as *The Geographical History of America* interrupted by bits of play or jingles, or to have banal rhymes interrupt a novel or even an autobiographical account of World War II, as in *Wars I Have Seen*. Stein questions not only the conventional Aristotelian divisions of the genre, but also some basic assumptions about the logical, rational, and exclusively discursive nature of conscious thought processes. She demonstrates that the underlying mental activities and operations of prose and poetry really always coexist in the writer's mind. Although the writer usually suppresses one mental process or the other, this is an artificial convention and a conscious effort that Stein apparently felt was unnecessary.

Stein's mixture of genres may seem disconcerting to many. Bridgman implies that this sort of thing occurs because of Stein's supposed inability to carry a project through:

> The actual contents of *The Geographical History of America or The Relation of Human Nature to The Human Mind* reverse the title and subtitle. Relatively little attention is devoted to the "geographical history," while the two psychological conditions of "human nature" and "human mind" preempt the book. Possessed of one of those dualities that invariably stimulated her imagination, Gertrude Stein opened with some sixty strong and coherent pages of distinctions. But then her prose grew increasingly prolix until at last the expositional fabric unraveled altogether and concluded on a wavering note. "I am not sure that this is not the end."[28]

But this disintegration of expository prose and the mixture of prose and poetry is an outgrowth of some of Stein's major concerns. Stein's self-appointed role as innovator often led her to redefine the genre along non-Aristotelian lines of poetry and prose in "Poetry and Grammar":

> Prose is the balance the emotional balance that makes the reality of paragraphs and the unemotional balance that makes the reality of sentences and . . . prose can be the essential balance that is made inside something that combines the sentence and the paragraph. . . .
> Now if that is what prose is . . . you can see that prose real prose really great written prose is bound to be made up more of verbs adverbs prepositions prepositional clauses and conjunctions than nouns.[29]

The following is her definition of poetry:

> Poetry is I say essentially a vocabulary just as prose is essentially not.
> And what is the vocabulary of which poetry absolutely is. It is

a vocabulary entirely based on the noun just as prose is essentially and determinately and vigorously not based on the noun.

Poetry is concerned with using with abusing, with losing with wanting, with denying with avoiding with adoring with replacing the noun.[30]

Stein also tended to jettison literary labels for artistic ones—*portraits*, *still lifes*, *landscapes*. But an even more basic concept in her work remains, which precludes any definition of genre from dominating absolutely in her work. Her one enduring concern was fidelity to the present moment of creation. For her whatever was happening in the conscious mind at the moment of creation was admissible as part of the work. William Gass, in his introduction to *The Geographical History of America*, calls it "the stylized presentation of the process of meditation itself, with many critical asides."[31] Gass explains that some of the difficulties in the book stem from the fact that it portrays the mind at work:

> We not only repeat when we see, stand, communicate; we repeat when we think. There's no other way to hold a thought long enough to examine it except to say its words over and over, and the advance of our mind from one notion to another is similarly filled with backs and forths, erasures and crossings-out. The style of *The Geographical History of America* is often a reflection of this mental condition.[32]

As in most of Stein's work, the referent to which she is ultimately faithful is the "stream of consciousness," so she lets the reader see when the mind is distracted from discursive thought or narrative flow by bursts of lyricism, wordplay, rhyme, and poetic language. She even lets what is happening around her interrupt her train of thought. Wilder says: "One of the aspects of play that most upsets some readers is what might be called 'the irruption of the daily life' into the texture of the work. . . . She weaves into the book the very remarks let fall in her vicinity during the act of writing."[33] This desire to maintain the integrity of the present moment accounts for the inclusion of digressions about her work, her dogs, her plans for the next paragraph. It follows, then, that if Stein begins to rhyme words while writing a novel, as in *Ida*, the poetry produced should be included. If she is thinking in terms of drama in the midst of philosophical musings, she will include that digression in that form. (This is really not such a radical departure; the dramatic presentation of philosophical content is as old as Plato.)

In spite of critics who imply that Stein's tendency to wander from her established purpose or to abandon her plans for a work in the middle of a chapter shows confusion or lack of character, this is Stein's way of dramatizing the problem of the artist who tries to work only in the present tense, without memory. The preconceived plan of the artist has to be remembered to be carried out, and Stein rejected remembering as confusing. Perhaps it is a sign of her integrity that Stein subordinates that preconceived purpose to the continuing activity in her conscious mind and has no fear of changing her mind if her mind has indeed already changed. She even shows the reader the process of the artist's own interest in a project waning. Admittedly, to witness such a process can be intensely annoying if one has a mind used to categorization and consistency and a character that insists on carrying out projects, however foolishly conceived. But if one can put aside one's own habits of mind, it can be interesting to watch the human mind at work, which is what Stein most directly presents, not only in *The Geographical History of America*, but throughout her writing.

CHAPTER FIVE

"ANYTHING IS WHAT IT IS":

NAMING, ORDERING, AND LOGIC

I<small>N</small> *Picasso* Gertrude Stein wrote, "A creator is not in advance of his generation but he is the first of his contemporaries to be conscious of what is happening to his generation."[1] This also describes Stein, an innovator who participated in the making of the twentieth century. Her stylistic development led her from the rationalistic orientation of the nineteenth century to what she saw as the twentieth century's skepticism about science and rationalism. In *Picasso*, she wrote that "The twentieth century has much less reasonableness in its existence than the nineteenth century."[2] In that book Stein cites, as one of the "three reasons for the making of . . . cubism," the fact that "the belief in the reality of science, commenced to diminish."[3] Donald Sutherland, in his essay "Gertrude Stein and the Twentieth Century," explains:

> the nineteenth century was still interested in causes and purposes and explanations. It was dominated, if not by Evolution, under which everything, even if incomprehensibly, served some future purpose or other — contributed in some way to "some far-off divine event toward which the whole creation moves," at least by a sense of direction in History, whether Hegelian or Marxist or what not.[4]

The diminishing faith in science and logic is reflected in Stein's movement from a view of the world as rationally ordered, implied in the elaborate human typology of *The Making of Americans*, to a non-scientific and arational but immediate acceptance of the world as "simply present." Weinstein believes that "In *Tender Buttons* the Jamesian universe of flux and process is dramatized by the processual syntax; the description, the verbal embodiment of the object, is as plastic, as multi-dimensional and as protological as the objective reality itself."[5] Hoffman also sees the lack of rational order in *Tender Buttons* as representative of this century's view of things: "If Gertrude Stein was an inevitability for the twentieth century, then as products of the same age we can probably learn much about ourselves in her enigmatic works. The supposed irrationality of her writing may be no more than a reflection of our world."[6] The movement away from the assumptions of nineteenth-century rationalism toward a more modern view of the world as flux is reflected in Stein's abandonment of traditional syntax, according to Weinstein. He says, "Conventional English syntax compels its user to accept the model of a sequential, linear time/space realm that is not true to the modern . . . world view."[7]

Stein's gradual movement away from nineteenth-century rationalism appears not only in the disintegrating syntax traced in earlier chapters, but also in her changing attitude toward logical and rhetorical structures. If language was truly one of Stein's main concerns, then naturally definition and classification would be the logical processes most relevant to her writing, for they are two key components of ordering the world through language by naming and sorting objects.

Definition is a metalinguistic statement that links a signifier to a signified, creating a sign to be accepted and used in the language (or code). It ordinarily works by designating x as a member of a class or genus y, and by listing distinguishing features (*differentiae*) that separate x from other members of class y. Classification works by grouping entities into classes based on similarity, on shared characteristics. Classification is also important to language, since—as William James indicates—a word may be applied to a whole group of entities that may seem very different in some ways but yet share certain basic features. James points out that "consciousness is in constant change," and that "no state once gone can recur and be identical with what it was before:"

Are not the sensations which we get from the same object . . . always the same? Does not the same piano-key, struck with the same force, make us hear in the same way? Does not the same grass give us the same feeling of green, the same sky the same feeling of blue. . . . *[T]here is no proof that an incoming current ever gives us just the same bodily sensation twice.*

What is got twice is the same OBJECT. We hear the same *note* over and over again; we see the same quality of green. . . . The realities, concrete and abstract, physical and ideal, whose permanent existence we believe in, seem to be constantly coming up again before our thought, and lead us, in our carelessness, to suppose that our "ideas" of them are the same ideas. . . . [W]e shall see how inveterate is our habit of simply using our sensible impressions . . . to pass over to the recognition of the realities whose presence they reveal. . . . We take no heed of the different way in which the same things look and sound and smell under different circumstances.[8]

James discusses the implications of this for naming and classifying objects:

Men are so ingrainedly partial that . . . the notion that there is no one quality genuinely, absolutely, and exclusively essential to anything is almost unthinkable. "A thing's essence makes it *what* it is. Without an exclusive essence it would be nothing in particular, would be quite nameless, we could not say it was this rather than that. What you write on, for example—why talk of its being combustible, rectangular, and the like, when you know that these are mere accidents, and that what it really is . . . is paper and nothing else?" The reader is pretty sure to make some comment as this. But he is himself merely insisting on an aspect of the thing which suits his own purpose, that of *naming* the thing. . . . Meanwhile the reality overflows these purposes at every pore. [O]ur commonest title for it, and the properties which this title suggests, have in reality nothing sacramental. . . . But we are so stuck in our prejudices . . . that to our vulgarest names . . . we ascribe an eternal and exclusive worth.[9]

Stein's attitude toward these two basic principles of ordering the world changes in a way that is consistent with the stylistic development already explored. In her first obscure style, Stein uses definition and classification straightforwardly, but the difficulty of the tasks she undertakes challenges the power of logical structures to deal with them, so tautology, paradox, and circular statements result. In her second obscure style, definition and classification are used playfully, as Stein recognizes that language can be used arbitrarily. As Schmitz points out, "The world systematized and tabulated by discursive language (system upon system, one string after another) begins to collapse when the arbitrary basis of language . . . is scrutinized."[10] And in the merging of the two styles in works like *The Geographical History of America*, both a serious and a playful attitude toward naming and sorting exist side by side.

In the first obscure style, definition and classification are undertaken seriously to describe and order the world in a rational way. Despite the obscurity and convoluted sentence structure of *The Making of Americans*, its basic goal is logical: to define different personality types or "bottom natures" and to classify individuals according to those types. But because this encyclopedic work is meant to include all human possibilities for all time, it challenges the power of logic to perform such a feat. Circular statements often result because when presenting all possibilities, every possibility has at least one opposite possibility (x or not x). This is consistent with Aristotle's idea that "If it is possible for one of a pair of contraries to exist or to come to pass, then you may assume that it is possible for the other."[11]

In *The Making of Americans*, Stein often presents both a proposition and its opposite in the same sentence: "Each one in some way can know, each one in some way cannot know, each one in some ways does know, each one in some ways does not know of each one some one in some ways can know, some one in some ways cannot know, of each one some can in some way know" (p. 787). At first reading, this statement seems illogical, because it violates the logical assumptions that "a proposition is either true or false" and that "a proposition cannot be simultaneously true and false."[12] The result of coupling each possibility with its opposite, each positive statement with its negation, as in the Stein quotation, would seem to be zero. But the sentence is not illogical when considered as an enumeration of all human possibilities for everyone who ever lived, is living, or will live—exactly the goal of *The Making of Americans*. This kind of sentence reflects the difficulty of attaining complete knowledge and of making absolute statements about even one human being. This difficulty is reflected not only in the content but also in the form of the statement, which links proposition to proposition, clause to clause. (Of course, this tortuous way of making statements also functions to lengthen the syntax, as pointed out earlier.)

In naming all human possibilities in the world for all time, one would be constantly aware that each possibility implies its opposite, each human quality implies its potential absence. Awareness of this sometimes leads to apparent self-contradiction: "Angry feeling is coming, coming, not coming, certainly not coming to be in them in some. Angry feeling is certainly coming to be in them in some" (p. 774). But what looks like contradiction is really an attempt to create an encyclopedic vision that includes all possibilities. Because Stein desired universal application and eternal truth, she turned to general but all-inclusive statements, often mentioning all possibilities in one sentence.[13] Stein usually does this by repeating the same verb or adjective, modifying the meaning of the kernel sentence through changes in the surface structure: the presence or absence of adverbs like *not*, *certainly*, or *completely*, as in the above passage.

In her pre-1912 portraits Stein also makes apparently alogical self-contradictory statements, but for slightly different reasons. Ordinarily two contradictory observations of a person known over a period of time eventually would be resolved into a total conception of the person. But in her early portraits Stein keeps these observations in their raw state, preserving each individual moment of perception, including changes in both the perceiver and in the person perceived. This is consistent with her aim to present knowledge without memory and to deal exclusively with the present tense. Without memory, contradictions aren't resolved, because they are neither noticed nor remembered. The result is paradox or self-contradiction: "One is frightened in being one being living. One is not frightened in being one being living. One is frightened again and again. One is again and again not frightened."[14] Again Stein seems to be contradicting the axiom that a proposition cannot be simultaneously true and false; but simultaneity does not apply here, for Stein is concerned with minute changes in a person over time. In discussing Stein's portraits, Steiner also mentions the tendency first to supply an attribute and then to negate it by supplying its opposite: "If an attribute is essential, the opposite attribute cannot also be characteristic, at least not at the same time. And Stein uses not only simultaneous opposites but negatives to depict her subjects."[15] William James points out that because of change over time, "Every thought we have of a given fact is, strictly speaking, unique, and only bears a resemblance of kind with our other thoughts of the same fact."[16]

> Thus my arm-chair is one of the things of which I have a conception; I knew it yesterday and recognized it when I looked at it. But if I think of it today as the same arm-chair which I looked at yesterday, it is obvious that the very conception of it *as* the same is an additional complication of the thought, whose inward constitution must alter in consequence. In short, it is logically impossible that the same thing should be *known as the same* by two successive copies of the same thought.[17]

Because some of the distinctions Stein makes in this first obscure style are very subtle, some statements approach tautology, a distortion of definition in which the term to be defined is merely repeated (x is x) rather than placed in a class and identified by *differentiae*. The more abstract Stein's subject matter, the stronger this tendency appears:

> Certainly every one who is being is being living. Certainly some are certain that in being living they are ones feeling that being living is some thing. Certainly some being living are feeling that being living is something. Certainly very many in being living are feeling that being living is something. Very many are feeling that being living is a thing making of them ones being existing. [*The Making of Americans*, p. 809.]

Stein seems to say that everyone who is living is living, but in the last sentence, she makes a subtle distinction between being and living, so that this really isn't a tautology at all. When Stein approaches tautology in this first obscure style, she isn't parodying or rejecting logical structures such as definition and classification. She uses those structures to make very fine, almost imperceptible distinctions among abstract concepts, distinctions which perhaps defy the capacity of the language to express them.

With the tautology Stein also approaches a completely static utterance, consistent with her desire to deal only with the present. In a tautology the verb is a linking verb, so no action is implied, and as the predicate nominative renames the subject, the only meaning is reiteration of the subject, as in "A rose is a rose is a rose," which creates a kind of still point in the turning world of words. ("I am that I am," Jehovah's self-definition, is a tautology, the only possible way to define the ineffable.)[18]

Tautologies very often occur when Stein's subject is identity. In the group portrait "Four Dishonest Ones," Stein writes: "Each one is what that one is. One is what he is, he is not needing to be changing. He is what he is."[19] And throughout *The Geographical History of America*, the phrase *I am I* occurs in discussions of identity. But I am I is not necessarily a tautology, at least from the Jamesian point of view:

> If in the sentence "I am the same that I was yesterday," we take the "I" broadly, it is evident that in many ways I am *not* the same. As a concrete *me*, I am somewhat different from what I was: then hungry, now full; then walking, now at rest; then poorer, now richer, then younger, now older. . . . And yet in other ways I *am* the

same, and we may call these the essential ways. My name and profession and relations to the world are identical, my face, my faculties, my store of memories, are practically indistinguishable, now as then. . . . So far, then, my personal identity is just like the sameness predicated of any other aggregate thing. . . . But this generic sameness coexists with generic differences just as real; and if from the one point of view I am one self, from another I am quite as truly many.[20]

Of course, tautologies also lengthen sentences, one of Stein's goals in the first obscure style. But the use of tautologies before 1912 may anticipate Stein's coming to terms with experience immediately perceived, which is a concern of the second obscure style.

When Stein classifies personality types in *The Making of Americans*, the delicate nuances described are so subtle that distinctions between types of processes become evanescent, as in the distinction between "dependent independent" and "independent dependent" types of people. And in the following passage, what is the distinction between taking advice and not taking advice? "So then asking advice and taking advice is one thing and asking advice and taking advice is another thing and that in the same one in relation to the same other one. Giving advice and talking to some one is one thing and giving advice and talking to some one is another thing in the same one giving advice and talking to the same other one" (p. 772). How does "giving advice and talking to some one" differ in these two instances? (X is different from x.) The distinction seems too fine to see, unless one considers Stein's interest in the almost imperceptible changes in the same person and situation *over time* discussed in her lecture "Portraits and Repetition." What Stein may be implying here is that x_1 is different from x_2, when differences in time are taken into account. S. I. Hayakawa seems to echo William James when he points out that:

The object of our experience, then, is not the "thing in itself," but an *interaction between our nervous systems (with all their imperfections) and something outside them*. Bessie [the cow] is unique. . . . But we automatically *abstract* or select . . . those features in which she resembles other animals of like shape, functions and habits, and we *classify* her as cow.

When we say, then, that "Bessie is a cow" we are only noting the . . . resemblances to other "cows" and ignoring *differences*. [The word *Bessie* leaves out] further characteristics—the differences between Bessie yesterday and Bessie today, between Bessie today and Bessie tomorrow—and selecting only the similarities.[21]

Though Stein may appear to reject or parody logic in some of the sentences of *The Making of Americans* and her pre-1912 portraits, this is not the case. Most apparently illogical statements result from Stein's attempt to order the world, to state stable yet subtle truths about a pluralistic universe in flux, all done through the relatively static medium of words.[22] Stein's own awareness of the difficulties of making sense of the world through language is expressed in the metalinguistic comment below:

> I mean, I mean, and that is not what I mean, I mean that not any one is saying what they are meaning, . . . I mean that I mean something and I mean that not anyone is thinking, is feeling, is saying, is certain of that thing, . . . I mean I am not certain of that thing, I am not ever saying, thinking, feeling, being certain of this thing, I mean, I mean, I know what I mean. [*The Making of Americans*, p. 782.]

Some cynical critics might read this passage as a personal admission of Stein's alleged inability to communicate, but this statement should be read not as a confession, but as a general comment on humanity's universal struggle with language and meaning, the struggle to use words to tell someone else what one is thinking or feeling.

As Stein turned from the representational first obscure style to the more arbitrary style of *Tender Buttons*, she moved away from a straightforward, quasi-rationalistic use of logic and rhetoric to name and order reality. A playful, parodic use of the outward forms of rhetorical structures such as definition and classification appeared as the second obscure style broken free from the constraints of logic. Neil Schmitz maintains that *Tender Buttons* is a "moment by moment" record of the play of Stein's mind with the world, and he points out that

> . . . since the writer is not fixed, writing from a position, from a clarifying knowledge of the nature of things, and since the world (carafes, cushions, umbrellas, mutton, celery) is also in process . . . nothing can be named and then classified, given as real. Everything is contingent, changing as it moves and the mind moves . . . the denoted world collapses. . . . Words as buttons, fastening side to side, signifer to signified, become tender, pliable, alive in the quick of consciousness.[23]

The reader should approach Stein's use of rhetoric and logic with an awareness of which style Stein is using and what its characteristics and goals are. In the first obscure style, it is usually worthwhile to try to figure out what Stein means by a definition or classification, and to assume that she is undertaking those operations seriously. But when reading her second obscure style, one should be wary of measuring statements against empirical and rational norms because definition and classification in *Tender Buttons* and similar works are used playfully and arbitrarily.

Since naming (defining, classifying, labeling) is so fundamental to language, the arbitrary use of definition is probably the most revolutionary linguistic act possible short of coining one's own words. But Stein's playful use of definition also acknowledges that language is really a system in which the arbitrary couplings of words and meanings (signifiers and signifieds) have become accepted due to widespread conventional use. Roland Barthes points out:

> Starting from the fact that in human language the choice of sounds is not imposed on us by the meaning itself (the *ox* does not determine the sound *ox*, since in any case the sound is different in other languages), Saussure had spoken of an *arbitrary* relation between signifier and signified. . . . [W]hat is arbitrary is the relation between signifier and the "thing" which is signified (of the sound *ox* and the animal the *ox*). . . . [But] the association of sound and representation is the outcome of a collective training [and] is by no means arbitrary.[24]

And as Perloff puts it, *Tender Buttons* makes the reader "consider the very nature of naming."[25]

In *Tender Buttons* the relationship between sign and referent becomes tenuous, as an object may be defined as another object with which it cannot possibly be logically equated. One finds the form "*x* is *y*," but *x* and *y* may not be synonymous, interchangeable, or even in the same class. For example, in the "Roastbeef" section of *Tender Buttons*, one finds the statement "Coal any coal is copper" (p. 37). Both copper and coal are minerals mined from the earth and so are members of the same class. But this definition equates them, ignoring differences. When the subject *coal* is equated with the noun complement *copper*, the result is an empirically false statement. But in *Tender Buttons* the goal is no longer representation of external reality, and definitions no longer describe the world as it is.

Some "definitions" in *Tender Buttons* equate objects or qualities that are really only loosely associated, whether by contiguity or similarity, as in "A Shawl":

> A shawl is a hat and hurt and a red balloon and an under coat and a sizer a sizer of talks.

> A shawl is a wedding, a piece of wax a little build. A shawl [p. 27].

Some of these phrases are related to facts about the referents. A shawl might be used as a head covering or worn under a coat. But although a shawl might be red, equating a shawl with a balloon or a piece of wax obviously does not represent the world as it is. And although a shawl might resemble a veil, so the wedding and shawl might be associated (particularly in Spain), when *shawl* is equated with *wedding* the logical systems of categorization by class or genus which underlie the process of definition break down. An event is equated with an article of clothing. Beyond the associations underlying some of the phrases in the above passage, there is wordplay (*hat* and *hurt, under coat* instead of *overcoat*) based on Stein's interest in the words' associations as signifiers as well as signifieds.

Similarly in "Cups," *Tender Buttons* (p. 49), one finds: "A cup is neglected by being all in size. It is a handle and meadows and sugar any sugar." Here at least one distinguishing feature of a cup—the handle—is supplied. But because the part is substituted for or equated with the whole, a synechdoche results. In a conventional definition, the whole (the item to be defined) is described as the sum of its parts or distinguishing features; that is, the definition should be an equivalent of the term being defined.[26] Similarly, the metonymic association between a cup and sugar, which is often contained, measured, and borrowed in cups, is the basis for the definition, as the two entities are equated rather than just associated. Frequently objects that are merely related metonymically are equated, as in "A recital, what is a recital, it is an organ" (*Tender Buttons*, p. 38). Here two nouns in different classes, normally associated metonymically, are equated. Although an organ can be part of the recital (the instrument being played), a musical instrument is not logically the equivalent of an event.

Tender Buttons also contains negative definitions (*x* is not *y*), sometimes creating an empirically true statement: "Sugar is not a vegetable" (p. 9).[27] But often *x* is so *obviously* not *y* that the definition confounds the reader's expectations of logic and amuses instead. When Stein writes "The sister was not a mister" (p. 65), the rhyme and rhythm of *sister* and *mister* play against the semantic opposition of these mutually exclusive words. At least on the literal level, *x* could not possibly be *y*.

In *Tender Buttons* definitions often result in paradoxical statements, but here the purpose is playful rather than serious as in *The Making of Americans*. Sometimes, as in the first obscure style, contradiction re-

sults when Stein states a proposition and immediately states its opposite. In the following passage from "A Long Dress" in *Tender Buttons*
(p. 17), the pattern is *x* is not *x*: "a dark place is not a dark place, only
a white and red are black, only a yellow and green are blue, a pink is
scarlet." Here unresolved contradictions are blithely stated and left
unexplained to bemuse the reader. When is a dark place not a dark
place? No qualification is supplied. This resembles a riddle more than
a definition, and when reading *Tender Buttons* one should probably
keep in mind that many riddles are just definitions in a playful form.
(What is black and white and read all over? What goes on four legs in
the morning, two legs at noon, and three legs in the evening?).

In the above quotation, there are also statements that contradict empirical knowledge of colors. White and red are obviously not black,
either as individual hues or as combinations. Hues are usually mutually
exclusive labels (except for tenuous distinctions between adjacent colors such as red-orange). Yellow and green do not make blue, but green-
ish yellow; blue and yellow make green. Pink is not scarlet, though
scarlet might become pink if mixed with a lot of white. Stein has subordinated representation of the world as it is to the arbitrary use of
language when she breaks down the ordinary system of naming colors
that is used to label, describe, and sort objects.

Similarly, Stein confounds colors in the passage "Winged, to be winged
means that white is yellow" (*Tender Buttons*, p. 15). Again, she creates
obvious paradoxes (white is yellow) by contradicting common experi-
ential knowledge. She also uses the format of the spelling-bee response—say the word, define (and spell) the word—to set up the reader's
expectation that a bona fide definition is forthcoming. Then these expectations are undercut, as the definition doesn't really tell what *winged*
means, though one can see that an association between wings and the
colors yellow and white might be based on contiguity as the signified
bird is evoked.

Tautologies are stated boldly and directly in *Tender Buttons*, as in
"Veal": "Very well, very well, washing is old, washing is washing" (p.
53). Here, as in the following example, the repetition and rhythm of
the tautology function as closural devices: "Elephant beaten with candy
and little pops and chews all bolts and reckless, reckless rats, this is
this" (p. 26). In this second style, tautology does not result from a
subtle and complicated catalog of human types as it did in *The Making
of Americans*. Rather the tautology asserts that each object is what it
is, "simply present," to be accepted directly and immediately for what

it is, without logical definition or categorization. Defying logical substance in favor of direct experience—while parodying logical forms—Stein uses definition and classification to assert that language is really a somewhat arbitrary system at its origins and can be used playfully and poetically rather than discursively.

The Geographical History of America combines the goals of Stein's two major obscure styles. As in *The Making of Americans*, Stein writes discursively about the real world, but here the subjects are not people and character types but, rather, two "real" though abstract philosophical entities: human nature and human mind. To this discursive orientation Stein adds the concerns of her second obscure style, the poetic style of *Tender Buttons*, the concern with direct presentation of consciousness as it intersects with the present moment. But in *The Geographical History of America*, Stein represents consciousness wrestling with abstract ideas, rather than apprehending concrete objects as in *Tender Buttons*. The result is a philosophical meditation that is sometimes sober and logical, sometimes arbitrary and playful, and sometimes all of those things at once. The work shows us not only the human mind at work, but also "the human mind at play" (*The Geographical History of America*, p. 155). In this return to prose and discursive thought, Stein sometimes uses logical and rhetorical structures straightforwardly to name and classify. But the work mixes poetry and prose, wordplay and philosophy, and thus definition and classification are sometimes used playfully, though somewhat less so than in *Tender Buttons*.

The Geographical History of America is basically a meditation on the distinction between human nature and the human mind, a differentiation that is presented seriously, though obliquely, in an attempt to explain something about the world. Human mind is pure intellectual consciousness, whereas human nature is emotion, ego, self- awareness, and identity. Because the *Geographical History* presents rumination about these two terms, it shows the reader process rather than end-product, which would be a clear-cut and succinct definition and classification. Thus Stein ignores Cicero's dicta that every discourse should begin with a definition of terms.[28] Stein does not directly define these two key terms, but instead intermittently notes some concerns of human nature and of the human mind.

By *human mind* Stein means the conscious intellectual faculty available to humans but not to other animals, whereas *human nature* is quite similar to animal nature. Here is as close as the book comes to a formal definition of these two key terms:

The human mind is the mind that writes what any human mind years after or years before can read, thousands of years or no years it makes no difference.

Now human nature human nature is just the same as any animal nature and so it has nothing to do with the human mind. Any animal can talk any animal can be but not any animal can write [p. 116].

Much of *The Geographical History of America* is at least indirectly about writing, about the logical and poetic faculties of the human mind as it works and plays. Stein approaches the "definition" of *human nature* and *human mind* gradually throughout the book, slowly revealing piecemeal what the human mind can do and what human nature can do. Sometimes she makes these distinctions negatively (*x* is not *y*): "The human mind has nothing to do with sorrow and with disappointment and with tears" (p. 67). Stein thus distinguishes pure mind from emotion, ego, identity, and bodily sensation, the creatural part of human existence. Similarly she states that the human mind has nothing to do with memory, associated with identity or human nature, while the human mind exists only in a timeless present moment in which awareness of self and past fades: "And so the human mind is like not being in danger but being killed, there is no remembering, no there is no remembering, and no forgetting because you have to remember to forget no there is none in any human mind" (p. 64). When in danger, one is preoccupied with self-preservation; but being killed means the dissolution of the ego and oblivion.

Stein also states that the human mind can know "that if every one did not die there would be no room for those who live now," but that human nature (emotion, ego, identity) cannot know this (*The Geographical History of America*, p. 53). The human mind is pure intellect, untainted by emotional, physical, and egotistical interest in self-preservation. Stein slowly reveals these distinguishing characteristics of human nature and the human mind without using formal definitions.

Because the book represents consciousness grappling with abstract philosophical ideas (and because philosophical musings are often hard to follow), this work remains somewhat obscure despite the relatively conventional functioning of both combination and selection. Obscurity also arises because the book shows the alogical turns the mind may take on its way to understanding, as well as the mind's detours into sheer wordplay. This wordplay sometimes parodies logic and linguistic operations of naming and categorizing, while forcing the reader to examine the substance of logic itself. *The Geographical History of Amer-*

ica reiterates what *Tender Buttons* has already demonstrated: that logic isn't the only way to know. Therefore, demands for consistent logic throughout the book or assumptions that Stein fails as a writer when she is not logical are inappropriate. In imitating the movement of consciousness, the work shows that the mind is sometimes logical and sometimes not. In *The Geographical History of America*, the parody of and occasional refusal of logic, seen in *Tender Buttons*, surfaces again, frustrating readers who insist on reason. Stein does not supply easy answers to difficult philosophical questions, so readers must ruminate and meditate along with her.

As noted earlier, Stein defines human nature and the human mind only obliquely, by implication. But the reader's frustration may be heightened because Stein does seem willing to define not key or difficult terms, but terms that are obvious, self-evident, and not very crucial anyway: "But what is the use. / Use is here used in the sense of purpose" (*The Geographical History of America*, p. 58) or similarly: "It can have nothing to do with human nature that can easily be seen. Seen is used here in the sense of known" (p. 79). Humor arises here as Stein defines words obvious to the readers, while leaving them to struggle with the nebulous concepts of *human nature* and *human mind*. She also lets the readers see the difficulty of defining abstractions while defying their wishes for easy answers to difficult questions.

Sometimes definitions in *The Geographical History of America* do not conflict with either logic or empirical data from the real world but are so vague that the inadequacy of formal definition and of language to express truth become evident. For example, Stein says, "To understand a thing means to be in contact with that thing and the human mind can be in contact with anything" (p. 74). Here two processes (understanding and contacting something) are equated, although they aren't really identical. Even a key term may be defined so vaguely that the definition becomes inadequate: "Human nature is what any human being will do" (p. 76). This is an operational definition, but it is so open-ended that it is impractical. Moreover, an entity is equated with a process or a class of actions. Although this definition mimics the traditional form of definition, it is alogical. Perhaps Stein is demonstrating how difficult it is for logic to deal adequately with abstractions through language.

Sometimes alogical statements seem to grow out of the struggle to define and classify, yet counter the spirit of logic while retaining the form. For example, in the following passage, all members of the set x are defined as members of set x: "All who like china in America like

china in America" (p. 72). This tautology parodies the logical mind's
desire for categorization.

In *The Geographical History of America*, as in *Tender Buttons*, Stein
sometimes states that x is not y when x and y are so obviously dissimilar
that there is no possibility of confusing the two terms anyway: "Tears
are not the chorus. / Food is not the chorus. / Money is not the chorus"
(p. 112). Here the definition is lightheartedly abused; *tears*, *food*, and
money are obviously not in the same class as *chorus*.

Sometimes apparent contradictions are really paradoxes that seem to
have a logical basis when examined: "They call it a motive but a motive
is not a reason why. A motive is what makes you do it. But what makes
you do it is not the reason why you do it" (p. 123). Stein here distinguishes between motivation and rationale, reminding the reader that
human motivations may have nothing to do with reason. But more often
the reader struggles with a logical knot that refuses to be untangled.
For example, individualism, which is associated with the identity-
consciousness of human nature, is distinguished from communism, which
is associated with the ego-free human mind: "Individualism that is human nature and the human mind communism that is human nature and
the human mind and what do they go on saying so and not" (p. 55).
But on the next page individualism and communism are equated, despite the fact that these two entities see themselves as opposed, "Individualism and communism they are not separate they are the same or
else human nature would not be human nature but it is" (p. 56). Perhaps this is meant as a distinction between the theory of communism
and its practice, a reference to the idea that no ideal state can ever be
reached because of the competition, ego, desire to win and possess that
are part of human nature.

Sometimes Stein uses tautologies when discussing deep, mysterious,
difficult, or abstract entities that defy definition, are beyond logic, and
are, perhaps, beyond words: for example, she says that America differs
from Europe in that in America "when anybody is dead they are dead"
(*The Geographical History of America*, p. 70). Here the tautology expresses the finality of death in a secular culture. Also, in *The Making
of Americans* (p. 919), she says, "Any one having come to be a dead
one is not then being living," and "Any one in any family living coming
to be a dead one is then later a dead one." Death seems to elicit tautologies in Stein's work, perhaps because it defies definition except by
negation. We can label but not describe it, just as we can label but not
explain God.

The essence of poetry is similarly ineffable for Stein: "Well anyway poetry is poetry" (*The Geographical History of America*, p. 211). The tautology can also affirm that some things are "simply present," and that "anything is what it is" (p. 83). For example (p. 200):

What is nature.
Nature is what it is.
Emotion is what it is.
Romance is what it is and there can be no romance without
    nature.

Questions of identity, too, often lead to tautology because of the difficulty of defining the essence of a human being, a problem Stein had grappled with also in her early portraits and *The Making of Americans*. "I am I because my little dog knows me" (*The Geographical History of America*, p. 107) and "Which one is there I am I or another one. / Who is one and one or one is one" (p. 107). Even the human mind is ineffable, because it is impossible to know and describe: "To know what the human mind is there is no knowing what the human mind is because as it is it is" (p. 140). What Stein arrives at here is the limitation of language's power to deal with large questions, such as the nature of death, the human ego, and poetry.

Sometimes definitions are so general that the definition becomes only loosely linked to the term and might easily be linked to a number of other terms. For example, the following definition only vaguely delineates the referent: "Kidnapping means that they take anything away" (*The Geographical History of America*, p. 62). Similarly, the following definition of a play (p. 238) doesn't really distinguish it from a novel, short story, poem, or painting: "What is a play. / A play is scenery. / A play is not identity or place or time but it likes to feel like it. . . . / That is what makes it a play." When Stein says that a play likes to feel like identity, she's referring to the fact that actors impersonate characters who take part in the action the play imitates. But in insisting that a play is not identity, she emphasizes that it is literature and not reality, and that as writing it is a product of the human mind rather than human nature. Yet all this is true not only of a play, but also of a novel, and possibly of some poetry.

Here is another definition so vague that it becomes almost arbitrary: "When a great many hear you that is an audience" (*The Geographical History of America*, p. 80). Once a definition becomes this vague, it can apply to a number of terms, and it demonstrates that language is to some extent an arbitrary system. S. I. Hayakawa has discussed the arbitrary nature of fixed definitions for words:

Everyone, of course, who has given any thought to the meanings
of words has noticed that they are always shifting and changing in
meaning. Usually people regard this as a misfortune. . . . To rem-
edy this condition, they are likely to suggest that we should all
agree on "one meaning" for each word and use it only with that
meaning. Thereupon it will occur to them that we simply cannot
make people agree in this way. . . . The situation therefore, appears hopeless.

Such an impasse is avoided when we start with a new premise
altogether—one of the premises upon which modern linguistic
thought is based: namely, that *no word ever has exactly the same
meaning twice.*[29]

Stein says, "I think that if you announce what you see nobody can say
no. Everybody does say no but nobody can say so, that is no" (*The
Geographical History of America*, p. 171). She also says, "Define what
you do by what you see never by what you know because you do not
know that this is so" (p. 170). Here Stein contrasts the difficult process
of knowing with the direct experience of seeing, a process that defies
categorization or definitions which can be agreed upon eternal concen-
sus. She suggests that this is a more direct and therefore more reliable
way of apprehending the world than through rationality and logic.

Once the limitations of language's power to definitively name and
order reality become evident, the recognition that words can be used
arbitrarily seems to follow (p. 203): "What are words. / Any word is a
word." Moreover, "And what is what is what is what" (p. 238). Once
the arbitrary nature of words and logical structures is acknowledged,
these can be used freely and playfully, for the sake of qualities other
than their ability to name and sort the objects in the real world. It becomes possible to use words poetically.

Stein's intention to present "the human mind at play" (p. 155) is
referred to in the book, and she mentions the ability of definitions to
give pleasure: "How likely are definitions to be pleasurable. / Very
likely" (p. 170) and "Do I do this so that I can go on or just to please
anyone" (p. 237).

In *The Geographical History of America*, as well as in *Tender Buttons*, Stein plays with words, sometimes choosing them for their rhythm
or rhyme rather than their sense, sometimes creating puns and riddles.
As in *Tender Buttons*, in *The Geographical History of America* Stein
occasionally parodies the logical processes of naming and sorting, defining and classifying. In the following passage she parodies the attempt to define *x* and to distinguish what *x* is from what *x* is not: "What

is the difference between conversation and writing, oh yes what is the difference the difference is that conversation is what is said and what is said is always led and if it is led then it is said and that is not written" (p. 217). Here rhyme supersedes the desire to define, as discursive prose turns into wordplay. She also asks "What is the difference between anything and anything" (p. 86), and parodies the process of differentiation when she asks "What is the difference between as snow and as snow" (p. 86). Similarly, she says, "Nothing to do and doing anything is not the same thing because either one thing or the other thing is doing nothing" (p. 139).

Some definitions are made for pleasure and based on poetry and wordplay. The following tautology (p. 72) is really based on a pun: "In China china is not china it is an earthen ware. In China there is no need of China because in China china is china." And here is a paradoxical distinction that is also a double entendre: "What you cannot eat you can" (meaning *preserve*) (p. 82).[30]

Throughout Stein's career, her approach to naming and sorting, defining and classifying was sometimes serious (chiefly in her first obscure style) and sometimes playful (in her second obscure style). When she combines both styles in works like *The Geographical History of America*, logical structures are both affirmed and parodied, used for both work and play. Her consistent interest in these activities so basic to language demonstrates her enduring preoccupation with the nature of language and its boundaries, and her apparent belief that those activities are fundamental to the workings of consciousness.

CHAPTER SIX

ON READING GERTRUDE STEIN

R EADING Gertrude Stein is never easy, but she is easiest to read in
the essentially conventional prose narratives produced early in her career—*Things as They Are*, *Three Lives* (1905–6)—and in many works
written toward the end of her life when she returned to prose in a new
style that incorporated poetry—for example, *Ida* (1940) and *The Geographical History of America* (1935). Almost all of the writing of the
intervening years is very obscure.

But Stein's obscurity is not incompetent, careless, or simpleminded;
rather, it is intentional. Its structure can be analyzed and its development can be traced. Before 1912 Stein's writing emphasized syntax and
suppressed vocabulary. The resulting prose style resembles the visual
obscurity produced by analytic cubism during those same years. Stein's
second kind of obscurity, created around 1912, which suppresses syntax and emphasizes vocabulary, resembles the kind of visual obscurity
produced by synthetic cubism. Then Stein began to suppress syntax
almost completely by arranging words in columns and lists.

In the late thirties Stein put the horizontal and vertical axes of language back together and clarity reappeared in her work. But she did
not end exactly where she began. Her experimentation with language
led to an understanding of its workings that anticipated by several dec-
ades Jakobson's observation that similarity is the basis of poetry and

contiguity is the basis of prose.[1] When Stein did put those two operations of language back together, she returned to intelligibility with a
freedom and playfulness that might not have been possible had she not
discovered, alongside Picasso, that art can be arbitrary as well as ana-
lytical.

Gertrude Stein's obscurity has made her writing a fascinating enigma
for many. Critics have used several approaches to try to deal with her
obscurity. This stylistic analysis of Stein's obscurity provides a new
perspective on, and often complements, some of the previous approaches to her work. For one thing, an analysis which suggests that
each of Stein's two obscure styles is methodical, intentional, and an
outgrowth of her interest in *language* makes it unnecessary to look to
psychological or sexual material as the chief or even sole reason for her
obscurity as some critics have done.

Some critics have claimed that Stein's obscurity was produced un-
consciously. For example, B. F. Skinner in "Has Gertrude Stein a Secret?" tried to explain her obscurity by suggesting that she practiced
automatic writing.[2] Although Skinner's attack on Stein in this article is
usually dismissed as polemical, he does recognize that many of Stein's
works contain both discursive and nondiscursive passages. Skinner
suggests that automatic writing produced the *Tender Buttons* style, with
intermittent interruption by the conscious mind (such as that evident in
Stein's early experiments with motor automatism), and so posits the
existence of two separate Stein personalities manifested in her writing.[3]

However, all this speculation does not negate Skinner's contribution
in recognizing that some lines of the *Tender Buttons* style make sense
and some do not. Skinner refers to the interruption of what he considers
Stein's automatic writing of the *Tender Buttons* style by "intelligible
sentences," which he calls "conscious flashes." He describes the basis
for this distinction:

> We first divide the writings of Gertrude Stein into two parts on the
> basis of their ordinary intelligibility. I do not contend that this is a
> hard and fast line, but it is a sufficiently real one for most persons.
> It does not, it is to be understood, follow the outlines of her works.
> We then show that the unintelligible part has the characteristics of
> the automatic writing produced by Miss Stein in her early psycho-
> logical experiments, and from this and many other considerations
> we conclude that our division of the work into two parts is real
> and valid and that one part is automatic in nature.[4]

Although Skinner's division of Stein's work into two parts is valuable,
his basis for distinguishing one part from the other is vague and subjective. A better understanding of the nature of her obscurity is needed.

As for Skinner's theory about automatic writing, it is possible that Stein's early experiments first revealed to her the nondiscursive, arbitrary, and associative possibilities of language some twenty years prior to similar discoveries by the surrealists. Stein produced the kind of writing Skinner is suspicious of (the poetic style of *Tender Buttons*) years later, in 1912, perhaps when cubism and other influences in the art world lent increasing validity to arbitrary associative use of the signifying elements. Only then did Stein begin to consciously produce associative prose.[5]

Another psychological approach to Stein is Allegra Stewart's *Gertrude Stein and the Present*, which uses Jungian psychology to explicate Stein's *Tender Buttons* and *Dr. Faustus Lights the Lights*, although Stewart admits "there is little direct evidence that Jung influenced Gertrude Stein."[6] Her theory posits a unifying relationship in *Tender Buttons* based on etymological roots of the words found there. She suggests that there is a relationship between the root word of *carafe*, the first noun in *Tender Buttons*, and the Arabic word *gharrafa*, a drinking vessel.[7] She notes that this word "contains the letters *ghar* which happen to be identical with the primitive Indo-European root GHAR, meaning to shine, glare, or glow" and is related to the English word *glass*. Stewart chooses to "leave aside . . . the obvious difficulty" that "GHAR is an Indo-European root while *gharafa* is an Arabic (Semitic) word"[8] and concludes Stein is suggesting that the parent word of carafe is *ghar*. Stewart also supposes that the question of whether there was "an original language that was the common ancestor of the Semitic and Indo-European families . . . could not have failed to interest a modern Jewish writer, at home in both traditions."[9] (Her assumption that Stein was a Hebrew scholar is not demonstrably true.) Stewart then traces a whole complex of words in *Tender Buttons* related to the seven primitive roots that have the form *ghar*: "(1) to shine, glare, or glow; (2) to rejoice or yearn; (3) to be yellow or green; (4) to yell, groan, or sing; (5) to rub, grind, or smear; (6) to bend or wind about; and (7) to seize, hold, or contain."[10] She then glosses *Tender Buttons* by tracing words related to these seven meanings (including images of glass, green and yellow objects, and enclosures).

The weakness of Stewart's theory is that this system is so complex that to account for its existence in such a seemingly random work as *Tender Buttons*, one must presuppose either a tremendous conscious effort that seems beyond human possibility or an unconscious manifestation of Jungian archetypes. She says: "Now . . . all this seems incredibly cunning — much too complex in its contrivance. But this kind of multiple meaning and overdetermination . . . is . . . what we find whenever the unconscious mind is active."[11] Her explanation is that Stein's "unconscious daemon often aided her with . . . that subtle and witty grasp of linguistic relationships and depth of verbal meaning."[12] Stewart's theory presumes that Stein's subconscious had a large role in the creation of *Tender Buttons*, though she does not suggest that automatic writing was involved: "I have attempted in my discussion of *Tender Buttons* to do justice to the presence of a keen, commanding intellect, which Stein certainly had. But I have also assumed that the writer's unconscious mind was exceptionally active — active . . . to a degree rarely encountered in purely literary work."[13] But what would Stewart say to Brinnin's report that Gertrude Stein, in her experimental work in psychology under William James, "announced that she had no subconscious reaction at all, and no one was able to disprove her"?[14]

Stewart also assumes that Jungian psychology is important in a reading of Gertrude Stein. She states that in *Tender Buttons* "one finds constellations of archetypal symbols (or rather veiled verbal suggestions of these) which indicate that the unconscious at work here is not mechanically betraying itself, as in automatic writing, but is moving toward unified solutions and creative discoveries."[15] According to Stewart "[s]uch considerations . . . suggest the mandala," which, "as the reader of Jungian psychology knows, is an instrument in the integration and transmutation of the self," "a 'magic circle' or enclosure for the unconscious mind . . . elaborated with more or less conscious purpose," and in part is "an arrangement of symbols from the unconscious."[16] Unfortunately, unless one accepts Jungian psychology and/or its relevance to Stein's writing, that part of Stewart's theory is not useful.

At best one must be cautious about Stewart's interpretation of *Tender Buttons*. It is based on an etymological root with so many associated meanings one suspects that on this basis many words could be arbitrarily linked. Beginning with another root, could one find the same wealth of interrelationships? Until that is known, the validity of Stewart's assumptions about Jungian psychology seems questionable. But Stewart's approach *is* valuable in its attention to word choice and to interrelationships among words. Perhaps the relationship Stewart sees results from Stein's conscious interest in language and word choice, and from her choice of subject matter as well. Much of Stein's subject matter in *Tender Buttons* is food and vegetation (things that are green or yellow); and it also contains allusions to glass in the section on objects and enclosures in "Rooms."

Another approach to Stein's obscurity has been to explain it as a veil for personal and sexual content. Interest in sexual issues in Stein criticism may have been stimulated by the belated publication, in 1950, of Stein's *Things as They Are*,[17] a story of a Lesbian triangle, which Stein wrote in 1903,[18] and which Bridgman and others believe to be autobiographical.[19] Edmund Wilson, in his review of *Things as They Are* written in 1951, sees Stein's sexual subject matter as a cause of her obscurity.

> The reviewer had occasion some years ago to go through Miss Stein's work chronologically, and he came to the conclusion at that time that the vagueness that began to blur it from about 1910 on and the masking by unexplained metaphors that later made it seem opaque, though partly the result of an effort to emulate modern painting, were partly also due to a need imposed by the problem of writing about relationships between women of a kind that the standards of that era would not have allowed her to describe more explicitly. It seemed obvious that her queer little prose poems did often deal with subjects of this sort.[20]

But Wilson very soon modified his view. The following note is appended to his 1951 review:

> I may have exaggerated in this review the Lesbian aspect of Gertrude Stein's obscurity. At any rate, the first volume of her unpublished writings in the Yale University Library—brought out since this article was written—which consists of prose poems composed in the years 1908–12, does not seem to bear out my theory. One feels rather that the ruminative dimness is a result of an increasing remoteness in her personal relationships.[21]

However, Wilson still insists on emphasizing Stein's private life over literary experimentation as the raison d'etre of Stein's obscurity.

Richard Bridgman also often approaches Stein's obscurity by explaining it in terms of hidden sexual content. Even though he mentions abandoning the goal with which he began his work on Stein, "to decipher even the most resistant of her works,"[22] vestiges of that desire appear in his biographical and sexual interpretations of her writing. See for example his interpretation of Stein's "Lifting Belly,"[23] which he characterizes as a lurid "erotic work": "Names again shift bewilderingly, although certain ones have a steady relevance. . . . External evidence attests that 'Pussy' is Alice Toklas, as in 'Pussy how pretty you are' ('Lifting Belly,' BTV, 78). . . . Other names of uncertain application appear. . . . But it does not require much ingenuity to decide who 'fattuski' and 'Mount Fatty' are ('Lifting Belly,' BTV, 86, 97)."[24] Bridgman and others sometimes approach Stein's work through biographical and often sexual data. This approach has varying degrees of success, depending on whether the critic avoids overinterpretation and on whether the critic either uses biography to shed light on literature or the reverse.

One of the most convincing readings of lesbian content in Stein's writing appears in some of Linda Simon's glosses in the appendix of *The Biography of Alice B. Toklas*, probably because many of the lines she explicates are relatively straightforward. Yet even Simon's glosses seem unconvincing when she tackles Stein's apparently private and idiosyncratic use of words like *Caesar* and *cow*.[25] The search for hidden erotic content can lead a critic to overinterpret a text (as can any approach if overzealously applied).

Although Elizabeth Fifer glosses several of Stein's writings as "erotic works" that "are demonstrations of disguised autobiography,"[26] her explications are plausible when the passages in question are relatively accessible and public. But as Fifer tries to decode what she asserts to be Stein's "hidden language,"[27] her explications become less convincing. For example, she glosses a phrase from Stein's *As Fine as Melanctha*:

> "Call it a lamb call it an unpronounceable residence call it peacefully, call it with stretches call it with withered . . . butter joy . . . obey it in leisure and earn and earn nevertheless gentleman." (P. [Possessive] C.[Case], p. 135.) One interpretation of this passage might have the "lamb" refering to the innocence of their relationship, an innocence Stein also explores elsewhere with her use of baby talk and her parodic romanticism. As their house is "not mentioned anywhere," it is also "unpronounceable," "residence" has attached to it frequent and vague associations with the idea of the sexual organ. Other references in this passage deal with the couple's age, emotions, and attitudes about sex. "Butter," like cake and water, appears frequently as part of Stein's special food imagery for sex. Sexual and creative urges come together in "leisure"—both are productive and should earn her respect.[28]

Is the evidence supplied really sufficient to support Fifer's gloss?

Perloff, too, finds sexual material in Stein. Of "A Substance in a Cushion" in *Tender Buttons* she writes: "The 'substance in a cushion' can refer to a woman's genetalia, and 'a violent kind of delightedness' then turns out to be sexual pleasure."[29]

That Stein's obscurity grew out of her interest in language is an alternative, or at least a complement, to the assumption that her obscurity is always an attempt to hide sexual content. That it is artistically, not just personally, motivated should also be considered. Belief that Stein's obscurity is entirely motivated by the sexual nature of the content fails to explain why there is more than one type of unintelligiblity in Stein or why Stein is obscure even when writing about sexually neutral topics. In addition, as Fifer points out, Stein is often quite frank in presenting erotic content.[30]

The analysis of Stein's relationship to cubism suggested here is another addition to a list of earlier attempts to deal with Stein's writing as "abstract" literature and to compare her work with cubism. Sometimes this comparison with cubism was a facile attempt by critics to dismiss Stein's work. Brinnin points out that "Certain of Gertrude Stein's early critics were antagonistic and full of misconception about cubism, but they were right in assigning her a place in the cubist camp, even when they felt this was but the most convenient way to dismiss her."[31]

One of the problems in the comparison of Stein with the cubists is that what is meant by *abstract* is not always clear.[32] That her writing was abstract in two different ways—as were synthetic and analytic cubism—is not always understood.

Michael Hoffman's book *The Development of Abstractionism in the Writings of Gertrude Stein* (1965) is one of the key works that compare Stein and the cubists. Hoffman's stylistic description of Stein's work is an important step forward for Stein criticism, yet his treatment of Stein and cubism isn't completely satisfying. His definition of abstractionism is essentially the dictionary definition, "the act or process of leaving out of consideration one or more qualities of a complex object so as to attend to others."[33] That Stein does this, as any artist must, is obvious. But because this definition is vague, Hoffman uses the term *abstract* to describe all of Stein's work without making clear distinctions between *nonrepresentational*, *plastic*, *arbitrary*, and *abstract*, although he is aware of the development of diverse stages in her writing. When Hoffman compares Stein's writing to cubist painting, his distinctions between the two stages of cubism are not consistent and rigorous enough.[34]

Even Steiner's distinction between two meanings of abstraction as applied to Stein's writing and cubist styles is somewhat problematic. The first meaning of *abstraction* applies to "works with abstract subjects," which Steiner applies to Stein's first phase or "typologizing portraits" (due to geometricizing of the forms); and the second meaning applies to "works 'without' subjects," which Steiner applies to Stein's later portraits, "where there is no overt mention of the characteristics or attributes of the subject."[35] But it can certainly be argued that in Stein's second obscure style, her portraits and descriptions do *indeed* have a subject, but it is what Weinstein has called "the linguistic moment," the intersection of consciousness with what is perceived—which is, of course, an abstract subject matter (which is Steiner's criterion for the *first* meaning of abstraction and applied to Stein's first phase of portraits). And, as to the first obscure style, because the subjects are specific people, it could be argued that it is not the *subject* that is abstract, but the mode of treatment.

Even when critics correctly formulate the analogy between Stein's writing and cubism, they often conclude that her adaptations of cubism were foolish, because what the cubists were doing was and is irrelevant to language and literature. For example, Oscar Cargill's analogy between Stein's writing and cubism makes the proper distinctions between the Stein styles and the cubist styles, despite his unorthodox terminology. He describes analytic cubism as "the 'fragmentary solid geometry' stage of Picasso's painting," to which he compares Stein's early "word-portraits" such as "Ada."[36] He refers to synthetic cubism as the "'plane geometry' period in Picasso's work,"[37] comparing it to "Susie Asado," which is similar to *Tender Buttons*: " 'The pot, a pot is a beginning of a rare bit of trees. Trees tremble, and old vats are in bobbles, bobbles which shade and shove and render clean, render clean must.' "[38] Unfortunately Cargill concludes that cubism is inappropriate and irrelevant to Stein's work. He feels that Stein was unwise to be influenced by Picasso, and that her works fail because of this: "Should not the present condemn her work to the degree that it appears constructed upon the analogy of experimentation in another medium rather than upon logical deductions in her own?"[39] Cargill feels that although "the present has no comparative standards save in painting for the judgment of her later work," it is questionable whether Stein "has properly defined her medium."[40]

Like Cargill, Brinnin also correctly formulates the analogy between Stein's writing and cubist painting, but he does it more precisely:

> Of the two modes of cubism—the analytic, in which the intellectual, geometrical, conceptual aspect of things was emphasized, and the synthetic, in which imagination, surprise, composition and lyricism were predominant—Gertrude Stein worked in the analytic period growing out of *The Making of Americans* and prior to *Tender Buttons*, when she moved into the synthetic phase.[41]

Although Brinnin defends Stein against the charge that she adopted methods foreign to her medium, he still labels her work a failure because she either did not recognize or knowingly discarded the essential nature of language by "destroying the connotative vitality of words."[42] He believes that Stein's "experiment was valuable as reconnaissance over areas that sooner or later had to be mapped, if only to warn others away. . . . But it is difficult not to conclude that she crossed the boundary line from writing to painting only to return equipped with means not proper to her subject."[43]

Steiner's analysis of the analogy, though much more sophisticated and useful than those of Brinnin and Cargill, also arrives at similar conclusions:

> It is ironic that Stein's portraiture broke down precisely . . . when it tried to make a translation of cubist technique and psychological theory into a medium that was fundamentally different from paint and canvas, and from "raw perception." Rather than serving as a key to cubism, Stein's writing illustrates the very real barriers between painting and literature.[44]

Although Steiner's criticism of what Stein attempted is sometimes well taken,[45] it must be said in Stein's defense that she does not ignore the differences between painting and literature, that her work should not be considered a "key to cubism," and that it has significance in its own right.

But what this analysis of two linguistically distinct styles of obscurity in Stein's writing suggests is that her adaptation of cubism in her own writing is quite relevant to her medium and that, even though words and pictorial images are very different, the operations of selection and combination are used similarly in the parallel styles of Stein's writing and cubist painting.

Furthermore, that there are two major kinds of obscurity in Stein's writing—one which is basically discursive (prose) and one which is not (poetry)—and that prose and poetry sometimes coexist in her writings has implications for the way in which readers and critics should approach her work. Some critics have suggested that readers need not look for sense beneath the surface of her writing. For example, Wendell Wilcox, in "A Note on Stein and Abstractionism," says of one of her poems: "The meaning we give it is only accidental. You as a reader are free to do with it what you like. The poem exists in itself and in its words. It is not necessary to do anything."[46] Donald Sutherland, one of her most enthusiastic admirers, gives similar advice: "Try taking the words as events in themselves. Or sit down and read. Forget this talk about her work and do not prepare to have an opinion of your own to tell. Simply read her work as if that were to be all."[47] This method might help uptight critics and readers enjoy Stein's words more, but for most it would require the kind of faith that personal knowledge of Stein seemed to provide for Sutherland.

At the other extreme, some critics have tried to find discursive meaning in each line of her writing, often ignoring her "poetry." For example, although *The Geographical History of America* contains some philosophy, as Stewart points out, it also contains a lot of wordplay. In Stewart's effort to discover the former, she often overlooks the latter. For example, Stewart explicates the following lines from Stein's *The Geographical History of America* (p. 192):

> Be is for biography.
> And for autobiography.
> No not for autobiography because be comes after
> So once more to renounce because and become.

Stewart sees these lines in terms of Aristotelian and platonic thought,[48] which may well be there, but she overlooks the puns and obvious references to alphabetical order as well as to the inside joke of *The Autobiography of Alice B. Toklas*. (The *Autobiography* is, of course, not what it purports to be, but instead was, in fact, written by Stein herself and can be considered either a biography of Toklas or an autobiography of Stein. Stein herself emphasized the latter.)

Harry Garvin's explication of religious metaphors and "recurring symbols" in Stein's *Four Saints in Three Acts* has a similar orientation.[49] Even though Garvin recognizes Stein's characteristic wordplay, he glosses the line "Saint Therese very nearly half inside and half outside the house and not surrounded" from act 1, scene 1, as follows: "Therese has no visitors around her ('not surrounded'). She seems at first a *little* more inclined to leave the house of God ('half outside . . . nearly half inside')."[50]

It isn't that anything is necessarily wrong with these interpretations, but so many alternate glosses of a given passage are possible that the worth of an elaborate interpretation based on such minimal cues becomes negligible. Here one tends to agree with Sutherland's suggestion that such glosses are "perfectly idle."[51] Although it is sometimes possible to discern obvious discursive meaning in Stein, because of her obscurity the critic or reader often has only minimal information and must be careful not to explicate more than that information can justify.

Although Garvin, Stewart, and even Steiner sometimes overexplicate Stein, their attention to etymological roots in Stein's writing is useful because it is appropriate to her concern with language and with word association (in a very learned form). Etymology is important in Garvin's gloss of the following passage from *Tender Buttons* (p. 22):

WATER RAINING.
Water astonishing and difficult altogether makes a meadow and a stroke.

Garvin explicates it: "During the night, a sudden hard (difficult) rain with thunder (an etymological pun on *astonishing*) and lightning (a *stroke*) reveals (*makes*) a meadow. *Altogether makes* suggests the unity and suddenness of the whole scene."[52] If this gloss seems convincing, it is because in this case Garvin has stayed close to the literal meaning of the words. But the following gloss of one of Stein's lines is typical of a tendency to project metaphorical meanings onto the text: "A white way of being round—perhaps a large feeling, or an idea for a poem, or anything that seems lovely, pure, complete."[53]

Steiner's attention to French/English puns in Stein's writing is an original contribution to Stein criticism. When these puns are relatively public and accessible, Steiner's analyses seem quite plausible, as in her reading of the last line of Stein's "Guillaume Apollinaire": "Leave eyes lessons I. Leave I. Lessons. I. Leave I lessons, I." Steiner notes the punning on the homonyms *eye* and *I*, and the correspondence of *lessons* with *laissons* (the French verb *to leave*).[54] However, when Steiner carries this approach beyond the accessible, the results become much less plausible, as in her gloss of the following line from the same portrait: "Elbow elect, sour stout pour, pore caesar, pour state at." Steiner's reading is:

The last two words . . . "state at" — seem inconsistent with the rest of the line, almost demanding the translation, "*l'état*." As soon as this is carried out, the last phrase becomes "*pour l'état*". . . . Working backward again, we shift the phrase "sour stout *pour*" to "*source tout pour*" or "*source pour tout*." If we interpret "Elbow elect" as "below elect," that is, elections from below, popular elections, we have "Popular elections, *source pour tout, pour césar, pour l'état*."[55]

In explicating discursive meaning in any Stein passage, the closer the critic stays to literal meanings and public connotations of words, the better. Before inventing elaborate metaphors to explain lines that do not seem to make sense as they stand, the critic should consider whether a particular arrangement of words has a rationale in terms of obvious and public wordplay, assonance, alliteration, or rhyme. In Stein's compositions, she often gives precedence to such considerations over considerations of discursive or symbolic meaning.

In Stein's first obscure style, discursive meaning can be found, but because of the generalized vocabulary it is vague, and the critic must be careful not to be more specific than the writer. In Stein's second style, syntax is often so radically suppressed that discursive meaning is impossible. In this style, there are often many sentence fragments as well as sentences built on false predication. Subject and predication are necessary in order to propositionalize. There is often semantic disjunction between subject and verb, adjective and noun. Critics have tried to find discursive meaning in Stein by metaphorical interpretations meant to reunite the disjunctive subject and predicate or adjective and noun, or by supplying a syntax. But either approach can sometimes put more of the critic than of Stein into the discursive meaning that is arrived at.

Critics and readers should neither assume that every Stein composition contains discursive meaning in every line nor dismiss her writing as devoid of sense. Rather, the approach should be tailored to the style of the individual work being considered, and to each particular line of that work, since Stein sometimes mixes prose and poetic wordplay.

Stein's name is sometimes linked with other writers of the twentieth century, especially Joyce, Eliot, and Pound. Those writers also use language in innovative ways and are difficult and obscure. But their obscurity is of a different sort than Stein's. Joyce, Eliot, and Pound all use words with an historic density and a depth of literary allusions. Sutherland sees the writing of Pound and Eliot as less modern than Stein's: "The school of T. S. Eliot and Ezra Pound is evidently of the twentieth century, but with their everlasting historicism, their infatuation with tradition . . . they are still not weaned from the superstitions of the nineteenth century."[56] On the other hand, Stein "insists upon using words as if they never had a history, in combinations never before realized in literature," as Weinstein said.[57]

Stein's writing presents unique and perhaps more difficult problems than those Joyce presents to the reader. Hoffman points out that Joyce's *Ulysses* and *Finnegan's Wake* provide the reader "a seemingly inexhaustible well" of allusions, but "the student of Gertrude Stein is offered slim rewards in this direction, for in her conscious drive toward abstraction, Miss Stein reduced the psychologic and mythic overtones of her writing to such an extent that their occasional appearance seems almost accidental."[58] Stein does not give the reader any clues that can be used to solve the puzzle of her obscurity as does Joyce with what Brinnin calls his "acrostic methods of mythological reference": "Joyce is bound by references; his technical puzzles can be solved with erudition, patience, and ingenuity. As Picasso supposedly said of him . . . 'He is an obscure writer all the world can understand.' Because she offers no references by which bearings can be taken, Gertrude Stein cannot be 'solved,' she can only be accepted."[59] The root of Stein's obscurity lies not in the meanings of obscure words or erudite allusions, but in the fact that she pushed language to the very limits of intelligibility in her apparently systematic exploration of its workings.

Stein herself recognized that her writing was unique in its own time. In *The Autobiography of Alice B. Toklas*, she writes: "She [Gertrude Stein] realises that in english literature in her time she is the only one. She has always known it and now she says it."[60] But some critics see Stein as merely a literary curiosity, rather than an important innovator. Purdy wrote: "Gertrude Stein belongs to the past now, and her words are generally unread. For most people the questions her work raised are now answered, and all negatively. There can be no literature such as that she wrote and defended; the novel, like the opera and the play, could not, and thus has not, turned in the direction she indicated."[61]

But with the advent of *le nouveau roman* and the theater of the absurd, Stein no longer is quite as alone in her writing as she once was. In "How to *Read* Gertrude Stein," Garvin points out that Stein shares with the French new novelists the "refusal of the use of the subconscious" and the "desire to cut away all the familiar associations and the cumulative excrescences of words."[62] Oddly enough, even Purdy admits that Robbe-Grillet's use of time in *Last Year at Marienbad* was anticipated by Stein.

> Gertrude Stein's three principles of composition are continuous present, beginning again, and using everything. Without commenting on the last I may say that the first two and their interrelation are very much her original contribution to the literature of our century; when Robbe-Grillet speaks of the "present perpetuel" of his film-novel, "qui rend impossible tout recours à la memoire," and creates "un monde sans passé," he is echoing her censure of "remembering," which causes "confusion of present with past and future time," and following, consciously or not, her example in the "looking that was not confusing itself with remembering," the *chosiste* example of *Tender Buttons*.[63]

Proust, Kafka, and Joyce are repeatedly cited as precursors of *le nouveau roman* by critics, as well as by the new novelists themselves. While Stein is too often conspicuously absent from such lists, her work also anticipates many concerns of the French new novel, as well as of the avant-garde in theater.[64] As early as the first decade of the twentieth century, Stein produced works that tampered with all the conventions the new novel and absurdist theater would later attack, and she even used some of the same techniques. The new novel announced the "age of suspicion" of narrative, plot, chronology, and character; but Stein, like Joyce, Proust, Faulkner, and Kafka, had already questioned these conventions.

Perhaps Stein's position as an unread literary eccentric whose judgments about the future of literature in this century were misguided should be reexamined. Carolyn Faunce Copeland points out that: "The year 1973 alone saw publication of at least three new works bringing together previously uncollected writings by Stein, and the reissuing of several previously published works, in paperback. Some new biographies also appeared. All this sudden activity amounts to a renaissance of interest in Stein."[65] Stein is less unread than she once was. The appearance of the new novel and the avant-garde and absurdist theater in the fifties, sixties, and seventies might well stir more critics and readers to reexamine Stein's writing. Schmitz points out that:

> Although she is still barely noted in most studies of modern narrative—Wayne Booth accords her a single reference in *The Rhetoric of Fiction*—Gertrude Stein's meditations on the subject . . . have become increasingly luminous in the past several decades. Her attack on the formal coherence of the novel as a false ordering of experience, on literary structure itself, no longer seems merely apologetic, a rationale for her eccentric style, her inability to work with established forms, but rather a lucid penetration of the *epistème* underlying traditional narrative. . . . She is, in brief, as perplexing as Alain Robbe-Grillet and William Burroughs, both of whom have similarly chosen to inhabit the "continuous present" in narrative, releasing their subject from the unities of plot and character.[66]

What once seemed shockingly radical and incomprehensible in Stein's work seems much tamer in light of literature produced fifty years later, just as the assimilation of cubist techniques by twentieth-century culture (Madison Avenue included) has made Picasso's art seem less barbaric and revolutionary. Stein herself commented on the slow acceptance of the new in art: "For a very long time everybody refuses and then almost without a pause almost everybody accepts. In the history of the refused in the arts and literature the rapidity of the change is always startling. . . . When the acceptance comes . . . the thing created becomes a classic."[67]

Stein shares with the new novelists and with dramatists like Beckett and Ionesco a basic skepticism about traditional narration and dramatic conventions. Like them she considered nineteenth-century realism not the only possible reflection of reality, but merely a set of conventions that, though comforting in their familiarity, are essentially artificial and by no means an authentic portrayal of the way people perceive reality in the twentieth century. Stein's questioning of the validity of traditional plot and character, the mainstays of both novel and drama, foreshadowed the skepticism of novelists like Robbe-Grillet and Sarraute, and dramatists like Beckett, Ionesco, and Albee.

Nathalie Sarraute announced in *The Age of Suspicion* that both the reader and the novelist have lost faith in the character;[68] and Robbe-Grillet agreed that "The novel of characters belongs entirely to the past."[69] Like these modern French novelists, Stein was also suspicious of the character. She said that people "lived and died" by the characters in nineteenth-century novels, but that intense interest in character ended with the coming of the twentieth century. "[T]here has been no real novel writing in that sense in the twentieth century. . . . Can you imagine anyone today weeping over a character? They get excited about the book but not the character."[70] Like these modern French novelists, Stein often portrayed characters as anonymous types who were often referred to only with pronouns: *one* in *The Making of Americans* and the early portraits, or *she* in *Many Many Women*. In *Two*, which Bridgman dates as 1910–12,[71] the main characters are known only as *he*, *she*, and *she*. So when Sarraute identifies the three main characters of *Portrait of a Man Unknown* only as *he*, *she*, and *I*, she was really unknowingly following Stein's lead.[72] Robbe-Grillet's characters are similarly anonymous. Sometimes they are identified only by initials as in *Last Year at Marienbad* or, like the narrator in *Jealousy*, may have neither name nor pronoun.

In *Ida* Stein further challenges the notion of character by creating a double or twin of the protagonist: Ida-Ida or Winnie (p. 338). Robbe-Grillet used a similar technique years later in *La Maison des rendezvous*, in which two identical girls are named Kim, as well as in *Project for a Revolution in New York*, in which there is a true and a false version of the character Ben-Said. In Stein's plays vast numbers of characters may each have only one or two lines, making it impossible to develop central characters in the traditional way. Butor's *Niagara*, which resembles a play more than a novel, is similar to Stein's plays in that it, too, presents a long list of characters, each of whom has very few lines:

	Luminous.	ARTHUR
	Full.	DELIA
	Dazzling.	BERTHA
	Wide.	ARTHUR
	With fringed petals.	CHRIS
	Shaped like great anemones	BERTHA
	Deliciously fragrant.	DELIA
	Geranium red.	ARTHUR
	Salmon cream.	CHRIS
ELIAS.	Sprung from a hardy crimson bud.	
	Turkey red.	BERTHA
	Abundantly flushed with pink.	DELIA[73]

Stein also rejected the traditional idea of plot, mainstay of the novel since the eighteenth century, and of drama since Aristotle. She felt the rejection of plot was an important trend in the twentieth century, pointing out that in the three most important novels "written in this generation, there is, in none of them a story. There is none in Proust in The Making of Americans or in Ulysses."[74] Years later Robbe-Grillet said that plot "had long since ceased to constitute the armature of the narrative" and that "to tell a story has become strictly impossible."[75] Like Sarraute and Robbe-Grillet, Stein felt that the expanding news media, as well as two hundred years of novel reading, had exhausted the twentieth-century reader's interest in narrative: "[Y]ou may . . . describe the things that happen . . . but nowadays everybody all day long knows what is happening and so what is happening is not really interesting, one knows it by radios cinemas newspapers biographies autobiographies until what is happening does not really thrill any one."[76] Sarraute also believed the cinema and newspaper had usurped the novel's traditional goal of telling a story:

> . . . if it is a matter of showing characters from without . . . and of recounting their actions and the events that compose their stories, of telling stories about them . . . the cinema director, who disposes of means of expression that are far better suited to this purpose and much more powerful than his [the writer's] own, succeeds in far surpassing him. And when it comes to describing man's sufferings and struggles plausibly, to making known all the frequently monstrous, almost unbelievable inequities that are committed, the journalist possesses the immense advantage over him of being able to give the facts he reports . . . that look of authenticity which, alone, is capable of compelling the reader's credence.[77]

As Stein's writing became more static, the traditional notion of plot disappeared from her narrative, just as it did later in the writing of Robbe-Grillet, Sarraute, and even occasionally Butor. In the theater Stein also tends to eliminate memory and present pure spectacle without much logical plot or action. This tendency to eliminate plot and dramatic action is also seen in Albee's *The American Dream* and Beckett's *Waiting for Godot*.[78] Kawin says:

> although Stein is concerned with psychology and Beckett with philosophy, the two writers approach the problems of time and language with similar literary tools: notably repetition in the continuous present. I am not suggesting that Steinese offers a resolution to the problems of existentialism, but it is interesting that their evolving attitudes toward beginning again and memory are so closely related.[79]

Stein's rejection of chronological order went hand in hand with her rejection of narrative or "succession in happening." Later the new novelists would agree with Stein that the convention of chronological order was not an authentic representation of the way man perceives the world. Butor asserts that "we experience time as continuity only at certain moments."[80] The digressive, associational mental time in Stein's achronological and even nonlinear works, such as *Ida* and *The Geographical History of America*, challenges chronology just as Butor did in his essays "Research on the Technique of the Novel" and "The Book as Object."[81] Both Stein and Butor challenge the nature of the book itself when they use columns of words rather than sentences.

Stein's abiding interest was in the present moment, where she felt all authentic perception took place. This interest in presenting each individual moment of perception led to repetition in her pre-1912 portraits. Robbe-Grillet's use of repetition is also notorious and similarly stems from an interest in the present moment. Like Stein, Robbe-Grillet felt that "an imagining, if it is vivid enough, is always in the present."[82] And, as Purdy has pointed out, it is this interest in the present moment that made both Stein and Robbe-Grillet interested in film. Because of this interest in the present, both Stein and Robbe-Grillet make idiosyncratic use of verb tenses, both staying in the present tense as much as possible.

Stein, the new novelists, and the absurdist playwrights—all of whom jettisoned the traditional ordering principles of narration and drama, such as rising and falling action and Aristotelian notions of beginning, middle, and end—were led to sometimes substitute arbitrary structures (whim, circular plots, and alphabetical order) for traditional structure. For example, both Stein's "Alphabets and Birthdays" and Butor's *Mobile* are based on alphabetical order. In *Ida*, as in many of Beckett's work's, the main character may act for no particular reason.

Despite some obvious stylistic differences among all these writers, it can be seen that Stein anticipated the concerns of the new novelists and the absurdist playwrights. It would be going too far, of course, to say that Stein directly (or even indirectly) influenced any or all of these writers. But in the century of Ionesco, Beckett, Albee, Butor, Sarraute, and Robbe-Grillet, it would also be a mistake to omit Stein's name from the list of precursors of many literary developments of the late twentieth century. As Garvin wrote, "The literary historian will have to remember Gertrude Stein when evaluating the originality, in theory and practice, of Robbe-Grillet, Nathalie Sarraute and the avante-garde writers and critics in France today."[83] Stein recognized, perhaps intuitively, that the future of twentieth-century art would be built on the foundation of cubism. But the fact that she also anticipated developments in literature and critical theory in the late twentieth century has, for the most part, been ignored for too long. Her importance warrants more serious attention.

The pleasures of reading Stein are not easy ones, but they are there. She should be read, at least in small doses, by anyone seriously interested in twentieth-century literature. Perhaps then she would no longer be dismissed as merely a patron of the arts or a literary eccentric, but would be considered a serious writer who had important ideas about language and literature.

PROLEGOMENA FOR A BIBLIOGRAPHICAL ESSAY

B ECAUSE THIS IS an interdisciplinary study dealing not only with Gertrude Stein but also with cubism, structuralism, and semiotics, it seems likely that some readers may be unfamiliar with one or more of these topics. For those who wish to know more, this list of suggested readings is tentatively offered as a place to begin. So much has been written in all these areas that it would be impossible to include here everything that is exciting and valuable. This list is intended as a personal sampling of what seems most basic, valuable, interesting, and—in some cases—relevant to the kind of analyses represented in the preceding chapters.

Things have improved since the days when Stein criticism was full of polemics and emotionalism. Much recent work on Stein has been quite good indeed. The really excellent articles are too numerous to mention, so I am limiting this list to a handful of books on Stein that are indispensable to Stein criticism:

> RICHARD BRIDGMAN, *Gertrude Stein in Pieces* (New York: Oxford University Press, 1970). Though one might occasionally take issue with Bridgman's approach, one cannot take issue with the overall value of this book. A really fine attempt to deal with the broad spectrum of Stein's canon, it is packed with indispensable

information. The value of the appendices alone—among them the first complete chronological listing of Stein's works—makes it most useful.

MICHAEL J. HOFFMAN, *The Development of Abstractionism in the Writings of Gertrude Stein* (Philadelphia: University of Pennsylvania Press, 1965). This is one of the first skillful analyses of Stein's style and her relationship with cubism. It is the foundation for many other works that pursue this analogy further. Hoffman's later book, *Gertrude Stein* (Boston: Twayne Publishers, 1976) also serves as an excellent introduction to and overview of Stein's oeuvre.

DONALD SUTHERLAND, *Gertrude Stein: A Biography of Her Work* (New Haven: Yale University Press, 1951). Although Sutherland's assessment of Stein is sympathetic, personal, and intuitive, this book is an excellent balance to the extensive negativism about Stein that preceded it. It contains many valuable insights about Stein's work, which — although intuitively arrived at and emotionally stated—seem to hold up well under close, objective analysis.

CAROLYN FAUNCE COPELAND, *Language and Time and Gertrude Stein* (Iowa City: University of Iowa Press, 1975). This offers a very intelligent reading of a sampling of Stein works. It was in the vanguard of Stein criticism of the late sixties and early seventies that saw Stein as a writer whose works deserved serious analysis.

In addition, the following works deal with specific areas of the Stein oeuvre:

LEON KATZ, "The First Making of *The Making of Americans*: A Study Based on Gertrude Stein's Notebooks and Early Versions of Her Novel (1902–1908)." (Ph.D. diss., Columbia University, 1963.) This is a good place to begin to understand Stein's monumental and monolithic work. Katz was one of the first scholars to draw upon the great deal of information in Stein's notebooks.

WENDY STEINER, *Exact Resemblance to Exact Resemblance* (New Haven: Yale University Press, 1978). On the whole, this is an excellent study; it is the first full-length study of Stein's literary portraits. The analysis of Stein's early portraits is good, although the later portraits are occasionally overexplicated. Steiner presents an intelligent discussion of Stein's writing and cubism, and an excellent discussion of the relationship between Stein's literary portraits and the history of literary portraits as a genre.

Among the biographical works on Stein, I suggest two:

JOHN MALCOLM BRINNIN, *The Third Rose: Gertrude Stein and Her World* (Boston: Little, Brown & Company, 1959). Not only is this an informative biography, it is also an intelligent treatment of Stein's stylistic development, including her relationship with cubism.

JAMES R. MELLOW, *Charmed Circle: Gertrude Stein and Company* (New York: Avon Books, 1974). This book is full of information, a pleasure to read (a best-seller), and refreshing in its openness about Stein's sexuality—an aspect of Stein's life often suppressed by biographers, sometimes owing to the insistence of Alice B. Toklas.

For the omission of many excellent books and articles on Stein, I apologize but refer the reader, not only to the bibliography at the end of this volume, but also to EDWARD BURNS, "Gertrude Stein: Selected Criticism," in *Twentieth Century Literature* 24 (Summer 1978), a special issue on Gertrude Stein, pp. 127–34; as well as to Maureen R. Liston, *Gertrude Stein: An Annotated Critical Bibliography* (Ohio: Kent State University Press, 1979).

The field of works on cubism is so broad that all that can be supplied here is a place to begin. The following handful of full-length works on cubism all present excellent introductions to the movement.

JOHN GOLDING, *Cubism: A History and an Analysis 1907–1914*, 2d ed., (London: Faber, 1968). A classic in its field, it contains perhaps the clearest analysis of the history of cubism.

DOUGLAS COOPER, *The Cubist Epoch* (New York: Phaidon, 1971). This well illustrated book, which was published to accompany a cubist exhibition at the Los Angeles County Museum of Art in 1970 and at the Metropolitan Museum of Art in 1971, presents an overview of the chronological development of the cubist movement.

ROBERT ROSENBLUM, *Cubism and Twentieth Century Art*, rev. ed., (New York: Harry N. Abrams, 1966). This book is another excellent discussion of cubism (with enormous color plates); it also treats cubism's impact on other twentieth-century artistic movements.

Readers might also look at EDWARD FRY, *Cubism* (London: Thames & Hudson, 1966; reprint, New York: Oxford University Press, 1978). This is a collection of writings by cubist painters, as well as early critical reactions to cubism by Apollinaire, Stein, and others. Fry's commentary accompanies each passage, and the whole is preceded by a valuable introduction to cubism. DORE ASHTON, *Picasso on Art: A Selection of Views* (New York: Viking Press, 1972), in the series the Documents of Twentieth Century Art, ed. Robert Motherwell, is an interesting collection of Picasso's cryptic comments on art. The recent catalog *Pablo Picasso: A Retrospective*, ed. WILLIAM RUBIN, chronology by Jane Fluegel (New York: Museum of Modern Art/New York Graphic Society, 1980), provides an opportunity for those who missed the recent retrospective exhibition to see the entire spectrum of one of the two key cubists.

Although there are too many books and articles on cubism to be listed here, in addition to the bibliography that follows, readers may consult:

> RAY ANNE KIBBEY, *Picasso: A Comprehensive Bibliography* (New York: Garland, 1977) and the bibliography of the John Golding volume, *Cubism*, listed above.

Providing a bibliography for structuralism and semiotics presents the biggest challenge, because an enormous amount of material is available. Perhaps the best way to begin is to quote the explanation of the relationship between semiotics and structuralism in SUSAN WITTIG, *Structuralism: An Interdisciplinary Study* (Pittsburg: Pickwick Press, 1975), p. 19:

> A semiotic theory attempts to understand signs and their use in the social world; it was suggested by Saussure as a science which would take as its subject the whole human system of meaningful signs and would contain linguistics as one of its divisions. As a theory, semiotics is broadly and powerfully explanatory, for it subsumes within itself a variety of explanations specific to certain aspects of communication: syntactic, semantic, pragmatic, meta-linguistic, meta-communicative. . . . Structuralism, on the other hand, is an explanation of just one of these aspects—the syntactic relation of signs to one another in a regular and structured system—and the production of that sign system by its makers and users. Structuralism, then, is a part of semiotics, just as linguistics is a part of semiotics, and it is frequently useful to distinguish between the two.

For a general introduction to the field as a whole, the best place to start is TERENCE HAWKES, *Structuralism and Semiotics* (Berkeley: University of California Press, 1977), a slim volume that provides a clear and concise overview of structuralism and semiotics and their relationship to linguistics, literature, and anthropology. Hawkes also introduces the reader to most of the major figures in the field and provides an excellent annotated bibliography, complete with suggestions on what to read and in which order. In addition, the chapter entitled "The Historical Development of Structuralism" in Wittig's book is a concise presentation of the key ideas of important theorists.

RICHARD AND FERNANDE DE GEORGE, eds., *The Structuralists from Marx to Levi-Strauss* (New York: Doubleday, 1972) is an excellent anthology that provides samples of some key theoretical works of the most influential thinkers in the movement: Saussure, Jakobson, Levi-Strauss, Barthes, Althusser, and Lacan. This anthology provides another valuable introduction. In addition, one might read ROBERT SCHOLES, *Structuralism in Literature: An Introduction* (New Haven: Yale University Press, 1974), and/or JONATHAN CULLER, *Structuralist Poetics: Structuralism, Linguistics and the Study of Literature* (Ithaca: Cornell University Press, 1975), for an overview of how structuralism can be applied to literary texts. For specific applications of structuralist theories to modernist writers (Stein among them), I recommend DAVID LODGE, *The Modes of Modernist Fiction: Metaphor, Metonymy and the Typology of Modern Literature* (London: Edward Arnold, 1977).

Given an introduction to the field, one should turn to some primary texts. Since Hawkes's annotated bibliography provides such an excellent list of these, I refer readers to that document and list here a handful of key primary texts most directly related to the approach presented in this volume—that is, texts which present the binary orientation of structuralism and semiotics to language and sign systems, an approach quite compatible with the dualistic distinctions so often made in Stein's own critical writing (e.g., poetry v. prose, diction v. syntax):

FERDINAND DE SAUSSURE, *Course in General Linguistics*, trans. Wade Baskin (New York: McGraw Hill, 1966). Originally published as *Cours de linguistique général*, ed. Charles Bally, Albert Sechehaye, with Albert Riedlinger, (Paris: Payot, 1915, 1922). This book is the cornerstone of the analyses presented here. Besides presenting a basic theory of the dualistic nature of the linguistic sign and discussion of two basic linguistic processes of selection and combination, Saussure states the case for extending the study of linguistic signs to nonverbal sign systems.

ROMAN JAKOBSON, "Two Aspects of Language and Two Types of Aphasic Disturbances," in *Fundamentals of Language*, by Roman Jakobson and Morris Halle, Janua Linguarum, no. 50 (The Hague: Mouton & Co., 1956), pp. 69–96. Here Jakobson presents his famous distinction between metaphor and metonymy—seen in terms of basic processes of selection and combination; thus Jakobson suggests that these terms might apply to nonverbal sign systems as well.

ROLAND BARTHES, "Elements of Semiology," in *Writing Degree Zero and Elements of Semiology*, trans. Annette Lavers and Colin Smith (Boston: Beacon Press, 1968). "Elements of Semiology" originally appeared as *Éléments de Sémiologie* (Paris: Éditions de Seuil, 1964). This is a very technical text, but a key work that is the first to carry out Saussure's suggestion and develop a theoretical basis and critical vocabulary for analyzing nonverbal sign systems in terms of structuralist theories about language (selection and combination, syntax and syntagm).

CLAUDE LEVI-STRAUSS, "The Structural Study of Myth," in *Structural Anthropology*, trans. Claire Jacobson and Brooke Grundfest Scheopf (Basic Books, Inc., 1963), pp. 206–17. Originally published as *Anthropologie Structurale* (Paris: Plon, 1958). Although the discussion of the Oedipus myth in this essay (the Greek myth and myth in general) is not relevant here, I list the essay because it, like the others, demonstrates the binary mode of analysis common in structuralism used by Levi-Strauss as he breaks myth down into bundles of meaning that are selected for their essential similarity and combined in making the myth and as he discusses synchronic (vertical) and diachronic (horizontal) axes of time.

Another group of works relevant here are those that directly relate semiotic and structuralist theory to art. Quite a bit has been done in this area recently, so again this list will be only a sampling of the field. First, here are a few theoretical works that help lay the groundwork for practical application:

MEYER SCHAPIRO, "On Some Problems in the Semiotics of Visual Art: Field and Vehicle in Image-Signs," *Semiotica* 1 (1969):223–42. This excellent article analyzes the signification of some basic elements of visual art, such as ground and frame, and how they affect the meaning of the imagery present.

LOUIS MARIN, *Études Sémiologiques: Ecritures, Peintures* (Paris: Éditions Klincksieck, 1971). Not only does this volume set forth a valuable theoretical discussion of the application of semiotics to painting (that is excellent for Marin's awareness of the dangers of facile analogies), but it also provides several nicely done applications of theory to practice (for example, his semiotic analyses of several still life paintings).

MIECZYTAW WALLIS, *Arts and Signs* (Bloomington: Indiana University Press, 1975), vol. 2 of Studies in Semiotics, ed. Thomas A. Sebeck. This volume contains a very lucid analysis of the application of semiotics to art, especially the analysis of the semiotics of architecture, a branch of the arts often thought to contain no content, only form. Wallis demonstrates otherwise.

JULIA KRISTEVA, *Desire in Language: A Semiotic Approach to Literature and Art*, trans. Thomas Gora, Alice Jardine, and Leon S. Roudiez, ed. Louis S. Roudiez (New York: Columbia University Press, 1980). This is a collection of Kristeva's essays, theoretical and applied. The influence of Lacan is strong, especially in the later chapters. The book contains analyses of paintings by Giotto and Bellini.

I would like to mention a few other attempts to apply the theory of semiotics and structuralism to art:

JACK BURNHAM, *The Structure of Art*, rev. ed. (New York: George Braziller, 1971). This study begins by discussing theories of Levi-Strauss and others relevant to this work; it then analyzes many paintings on the basis of distinctions between the natural and the cultural as laid out by Levi-Strauss in *The Raw and the Cooked*. It is very difficult to read; compare his jargon-laden analyses with the clarity of Marin's study cited above. Burnham's book has been controversial. See G. and G. Dorfman's reaction to Burnham in "Reaffirming Painting: A Critique of Structuralist Criticism," *Art Forum* 16 (October 1977): 59–65.

PIERRE DAIX and JOAN ROSSELET, comps., *Picasso: The Cubist Years 1907–1916: A Catalogue Raisonné of the Paintings and Related Works* (New York Graphic Society/Little, Brown and Co., 1979). In the text of this catalog Daix also applies some of Levi-Strauss's theories to the study of cubism. Like Burnham's book, the Daix and Rosselet text has also been controversial. See, for example, John Richardson's review, "Your Show of Shows," in *New York Review of Books*, July 17, 1980, pp. 16–17.

RANDA DUBNICK, "Metaphor and Metonymy in the Paintings of René Magritte," *Contemporary Literature* 21 (Summer 1980):407–19. This article applies Jakobson's distinction between metaphor and metonymy to Magritte's visual puns and puzzles.

Other excellent examples of practical applications of semiotics/structuralist theory to art can be found in the works of Marin, Wallis, and Kristeva listed above.

THE FOLLOWING LIST of works and dates of composition follows
Bridgman's "Key to the *Yale Catalogue*" in *Gertrude Stein in Pieces*,
pp. 365–85, except where deviations are noted.

Things as They Are (also titled *Q.E.D.*, *Quod Erat Demonstra-*
 tum), 1903
Three Lives, 1905–6
The Making of Americans, (1903,) 1906–11
"Matisse," 1909
"Picasso," 1909
"Four Dishonest Ones," 1911
Two: Gertrude Stein and Her Brother, 1910–12
A Long Gay Book, 1909–12
Tender Buttons, 1912[1]
"The Portrait of Mabel Dodge at the Villa Curonia," 1912[2]
G. M. P. (also titled *Matisse, Picasso and Gertrude*
 Stein), 1911–12
"Monsieur Vollard et Cézanne," 1912
"Mi-Careme," 1912
What Happened. A Five Act Play, 1913
"Susie Asado," 1913
"Oval," 1914
"Johnny Grey," 1915

"Study Nature," 1915
"Pink Melon Joy," 1915
"Lifting Belly," 1917
Counting Her Dresses. A Play, 1917
"Have They Attacked Mary He Giggled," 1917
A Circular Play, 1920
"A List," 1923
"If I Told Him: A Completed Portrait of Picasso," 1923
"A Birthday Book," 1924
"Composition as Explanation," 1926
Four Saints in Three Acts: An Opera to Be Sung, 1927
Lucy Church Amiably, 1927
"Before the Flowers of Friendship Faded Friendship Faded," 1930
"History or Messages from History," 1930
I-IIII (play), 1930
They Must. Be Wedded. To Their Wife. A Play., 1931
A Play of Pounds, 1932
Short Sentences, 1932
The Autobiography of Alice B. Toklas, 1932
Four in America, 1934
"And Now," 1934
Lectures in America, 1934
    "What Is English Literature," "Pictures,"
    "Plays," "The Gradual Making of the Making
    of Americans," "Portraits and Repetition,"
    "Poetry and Grammar"
Narration, 1935
*The Geographical History of America; or, The Relation of
    Human Nature to the Human Mind*, 1935
What Are Masterpieces and Why Are There So Few of Them, 1935
Listen to Me. A Play., 1936
Everybody's Autobiography, 1936
Dr. Faustus Lights the Lights, 1938
Picasso, 1938
The World Is Round, 1938
"To Do: Alphabets and Birthdays," 1940
Ida: A Novel, 1940
Mrs. Reynolds: A Novel, 1940
Wars I Have Seen, 1942–44
Brewsie and Willie, 1945
The Mother of Us All, 1945–46

NOTES

Introduction

1. Michael J. Hoffman, *The Development of Abstractionism in the Writings of Gertrude Stein* (Philadelphia: University of Pennsylvania Press, 1965), pp. 18–19.

2. W. G. Rogers, *When This You See Remember Me: Gertrude Stein in Person* (1948; reprint, New York: Avon, 1973), p. 42.

3. Norman Weinstein's *Gertrude Stein and the Literature of the Modern Consciousness* (New York: Frederick Ungar, 1970) is the first book to treat Stein's writing as a linguistic phenomenon, relating it to ideas of Benjamin Whorf and Edward Sapir. Although it only mentions structural linguistics in passing (p. 6), this book prepares the way for the use of structural linguistics to illuminate Stein's work. Wendy Steiner's *Exact Resemblance to Exact Resemblance: The Literary Portraiture of Gertrude Stein* (New Haven: Yale University Press, 1978) also draws on ideas from structuralism and semiotics in analyzing Stein. See, for example, Steiner's use of Pierce's distinctions among "indexical," "iconic," and "symbolic" signs, pp. 5–6. Bruce Bassoff's brief article, "Gertrude Stein's 'Composition as Explanation'" states that "Gertrude Stein's 'Composition as Explanation' is a kind of premonitory condensation of some of the salient principles of semiotic analysis from Walter Benjamin to Claude Levi-Strauss." ("Gertrude Stein's 'Composition as Explanation,'" *Twentieth Century Literature* 24 [Spring 1978]:76). Probably the most direct applications to date of structuralist theory to Stein's writing have been David Lodge's "Gertrude Stein," *The Modes of Modernist Fiction: Metaphor, Metonymy and the Typology of Modern Literature* (London: Edward Arnold, 1977), pp. 144–155; and my article, "Two Types of Obscurity in the Writings of Gertrude Stein," *Emporia State Research Studies* 24 (Winter 1976):5–27, on which chapters 1 and 2 of this volume are based.

4. That Stein's two obscure styles are based on the systematic suppression of first one and then the other of two basic linguistic operations—selection and combination—

is a conclusion that logically follows if one compares Jakobson's theories with Stein's lectures, which contrast the prose of *The Making of Americans* with the poetry of *Tender Buttons*. I explored this idea earlier in "Two Types of Obscurity in the Writings of Gertrude Stein" (1976). (See also my "Gertrude Stein and Cubism: A Structural Analysis of Obscurity" [Ph.D. diss., University of Colorado 1976].) These works attempt to relate Stein's writing to cubist and structuralist theories. David Lodge draws similar conclusions about Stein's writing and Jakobson's theories. He aligns Stein's notion of prose and *The Making of Americans* with Jakobson's similarity disorder and her *Tender Buttons* with contiguity disorder. (See *The Modes of Modernist Fiction*, [1977,] pp. 144–55; this idea is also mentioned on pp. 486–89 of "The Language of Modernist Fiction: Metaphor and Metonymy" in *Modernism: 1890–1930*, ed. Malcolm Bradbury and James MacFarlane (Atlantic Highlands, N.J.: Humanities Press, 1978), first published in England by Penguin in 1974. However, Lodge's brief discussion does not extend this idea to a comparison of Stein's writing and cubism; in fact, he maintains that *Tender Buttons* is surrealist rather than cubist (see *The Modes of Modernist Fiction*, p. 152). But the link between structuralist theory and Stein's literary practice has important implications. One is that Stein's obscurity is based on conscious exploration of the nature of language. Another is that, using Barthes and Jakobson's reformulations of Saussure's linguistic operations in terms applicable to nonverbal sign systems, one can identify phenomena in cubism's two phases that correspond to those in Stein's writing.

5. Gertrude Stein, *Picasso* (Boston: Beacon Press, 1959), p. 16. First published in French (Paris: Librairie Flourie, 1938).

6. The terms *analytic* and *synthetic cubism* are commonly used, though not without some controversy, the objection being that while they mark a distinction between these two styles, still finer distinctions can be made (such as hermetic cubism as a kind of analytic cubism, and collage cubism as a type of synthetic cubism). But the more familiar terms *analytic* and *synthetic* are preferable here because the broader distinctions are more useful. The emphasis on contiguity applies to all analytic cubism, including hermetic; the emphasis on selection to synthetic cubism as a whole. Similarly, though one might note even finer stages in Stein's writing, in *all* of her first obscure style contiguity is stressed, and in the *whole* of her second obscure style selection is emphasized.

7. D. C. Yalden-Thompson, "Obscurity, Exhibitionism and Gertrude Stein," *Virginia Quarterly Review* 34 (Winter 1958):137.

8. Gertrude Stein, quoted in "A Transatlantic Interview 1946," in *A Primer for the Gradual Understanding of Gertrude Stein*, ed. Robert Bartlett Haas (Los Angeles: Black Sparrow Press, 1971), p. 18.

9. Edmund Wilson, *Axel's Castle: A Study in the Imaginative Literature of 1870–1930* (New York: Charles Scribner's Sons, 1931), p. 243.

10. Gertrude Stein, *The Making of Americans: Being a History of a Family's Progress*, complete version (1925; New York: Something Else Press, 1966), p. 15. Subsequent references to this work will appear within the text.

11. Gertrude Stein, *Tender Buttons* (New York: Claire-Marie, 1914), p. 44. Subsequent references to this work will appear within the text.

Chapter One

1. See "Two Types of Language and Two Types of Aphasic Disturbances," in *Fundamentals of Language*, by Roman Jakobson and Morris Halle, Janua Linguarum, no.

50 (The Hague: Mouton & Co., 1956).

2. John Golding, *Cubism: A History and An Analysis, 1907–1914*, 2d ed. (London: Faber & Faber, 1968), p. 80.

3. Ibid.

4. Ibid., p. 114. But this terminology is not without controversy, as Golding points out in his discussion (pp. 114–17). The works of analytic cubism became increasingly difficult to read; thus the term *hermetic cubism* is sometimes applied to cubist works produced in 1910 and 1911 (ibid., p. 87). I mean to include such works in the term *analytic cubism*.

5. Richard Bridgman, *Gertrude Stein in Pieces* (New York: Oxford University Press, 1970), p. 365. Bridgman supplies date of composition.

6. Ibid., p. 366.

7. Golding, p. 114. The critical terminology applied to cubism is far from uniform. For example, Edward Fry distinguishes the *papiers collés* and *collage cubism* of 1912–13 from the paintings produced a few years later, which he refers to as *synthetic cubism* (Edward Fry, "Introduction," *Cubism* [1966; reprint; New York : Oxford University Press, 1978], p. 33). I will be following more general usage by including the cubist collages when referring to synthetic cubism. The stylistic tendencies relevant to this discussion appear in the collages of 1912 as well as in the paintings that followed.

8. Golding, p. 103.

9. Ibid., p. 120.

10. Ibid., pp. 107–9, 112.

11. Bridgman, pp. 366–67.

12. Of course, this was not a completely new idea. Matisse and the Fauves had used color arbitrarily and nonrealistically as early as 1904 (Fry, p. 12). Even in cubism this idea developed over time. Fry points out that as early as 1910 some of the cubist facets began to be used with "an artistic logic of their own, as much in accordance with the rhythmic structure of the painting as with the necessity of describing the subject" (p. 19).

13. Date provided in editor's note preceding "What Is English Literature," in Gertrude Stein, *Writings and Lectures 1909–1945*, ed. Patricia Meyerowitz (1967; Baltimore: Penguin Books, 1971), p. 31.

14. Gertrude Stein, "Poetry and Grammar," *Lectures in America* (Boston: Beacon Press, 1935), p. 228.

15. Ibid., p. 230.

16. Ibid., pp. 230–31.

17. Roland Barthes, "Elements of Semiology," in *Writing Degree Zero and Elements of Semiology*, trans. Annette Lavers and Colin Smith (Boston: Beacon Press, 1967), p. 58. Originally published as *Éléments de Sémiologie* (Paris: Éditions de Seuil, 1964).

18. Ibid., p. 59. (Barthes is quoting Saussure, *Cours de linguistique générale*, p. 170.)

19. Roland Barthes, "Writing Degree Zero," ibid., pp. 46–47. Originally published as *Le Degré zéro de l'écriture* (Paris: Editions de Seuil, 1953).

20. Ibid., p. 48.

21. Roman Jakobson, *Studies on Child Language and Aphasia*, Janua Linguarum, minor series, no. 114 (The Hague: Mouton & Co., 1971), p. 73.

22. Ronald Levinson, "Gertrude Stein, William James, and Grammar," *American Journal of Psychology* 54 (Jan. 1941):124–28.

23. William James, *Psychology: Briefer Course* (New York: Henry Holt & Co.,

1892), p. 160.

24. Levinson, p. 126.

25. Ibid., p. 127. See also Steiner's discussion of James's ideas about transitive and substantive parts of speech and the relationship of these ideas to Stein's style, pp. 55–58.

26. Jakobson, *Studies on Child Language and Aphasia*, pp. 63–64.

27. See James, pp. 264–65.

28. Ibid., p. 267.

29. Ibid., p. 269.

30. Robert Haas, "Another Garland for Gertrude Stein," in *What Are Masterpieces*, by Gertrude Stein (New York: Pitman Publishing Corp., 1940), p. 21.

31. Roman Jakobson, "Two Aspects of Language and Two Types of Aphasic Disturbances." That two types of obscurity result from suppression of each of two linguistic operations was observed by Jakobson in the course of his work on aphasia. The significance of this work and of Jakobson's *Studies on Child Language and Aphasia* in an analysis of Stein's writing lies not in the discussion of aphasia per se, but rather in the structural analysis of language contained in these works. On page 76 of *Studies on Child Language and Aphasia*, Jakobson states, "The study of aphasia requires the structural analysis of language." In using Jakobson's theories, I do not intend any implication that Stein suffered from aphasia. In aphasia the suppression of either of the two linguistic operations of contiguity or similarity is entirely involuntary and pathological, whereas Stein's theoretical writings indicate that each of her two obscure styles was created quite consciously for certain aesthetic and theoretical reasons—all arguments about "automatic writing" to the contrary.

32. Stein, "Poetry and Grammar," pp. 210–11. In her interest in syntax and grammar, Stein concentrates on an aspect of language that would later became central in work of transformational linguists like Noam Chomsky.

33. Ibid., p. 223.

34. Gertrude Stein, "The Gradual Making of *The Making of Americans*," in *Lectures in America*, p. 147.

35. Stein, "Poetry and Grammar," p. 221.

36. Hoffman, pp. 77–78.

37. Ibid., p. 81.

38. Ibid., p. 133.

39. Ibid., p. 138.

40. Neil Schmitz, "Portrait, Patriarch, and Mythos: The Revenge of Stein," *Salmagundi* 40 (Winter 1978):77.

41. Bridgman, p. 74.

42. Stein, "The Gradual Making of *The Making of Americans*," p. 147.

43. Jakobson, *Studies on Child Language and Aphasia*, p. 54.

44. Ibid., p. 57.

45. Ibid., pp. 69–70.

46. See Steiner's interesting chapter, "Literary Cubism: The Limits of the Analogy" in her *Exact Resemblance to Exact Resemblance*, pp. 131–60. See also John Malcolm Brinnin, *The Third Rose: Gertrude Stein and Her World* (Boston: Little, Brown, 1959), p. 134.

47. Brinnin, p. 70.

48. Ibid., p. 71.

49. Gertrude Stein, quoted in "A Transatlantic Interview 1946," in *A Primer for the*

Gradual Understanding of Gertrude Stein, ed. Robert Bartlett Haas (Los Angeles: Black Sparrow Press, 1971), p. 17.

50. James R. Mellow, *Charmed Circle: Gertrude Stein & Company* (New York: Avon Books, 1974), p. 114.

51. Rogers, p. 53.

52. Mellow, p. 121.

53. Ibid., 114.

54. Rogers, p. 55.

55. Brinnin, p. 81.

56. Leon Katz and Edward Burns, "'They Walk in the Light': Gertrude Stein and Pablo Picasso," in *Gertrude Stein on Picasso*, ed. Edward Burns (New York: Liveright, 1970), pp. 109–10.

57. Stein, *Picasso*, p. 16.

58. Leo Stein, *Journey into the Self: Being the Letters, Papers, and Journals of Leo Stein*, ed. Edmund Fuller (New York: Crown Publishers, 1950), p. 53. The quote appears in a letter to Mable Weeks dated February 7, 1913. (Bridgman's dating of this letter as 1911 is apparently in error.)

59. Arnold Ronnebeck, "Gertrude Was always Giggling," *Books Abroad* 19 (Winter 1945):3.

60 Brinnin, p. 164.

61. In fact, Schmitz suggests that, like Leo, Picasso represented a dominant patriarchal force in Stein's life that she ultimately escaped. "Portrait, Patriarchy, Mythos: The Revenge of Gertrude Stein," p. 72.

62. For example, Steiner (p. 140) points out some interesting similarities between James's ideas about perception and Cézanne's ideas on the same subject. Timothy Mitchell points out that Bergson's ideas about perception were very much in the air in Paris at the time and were reflected in the writing of the cubist painters. Perhaps it is even possible that Stein herself was influenced by Bergson's ideas (via the cubists). See Timothy Mitchell, "Bergson, Le Bon and Hermetic Cubism," in *Journal of Aesthetics and Art Criticism* 36 (Winter 1977):177.

63. For a very fine discussion of the history of the literary portrait and Stein's place in the history of that genre, see the chapter entitled "The Literary Portrait: History and Theory" in Steiner, *Exact Resemblance to Exact Resemblance*.

64. Stein quoted in "A Transatlantic Interview 1946," p. 15.

65. Stein, *Picasso*, p. 11.

66. William Barrett, *Irrational Man: A Study in Existential Philosophy* (New York: Doubleday & Co., 1958), p. 50.

67. Ibid., p. 54.

68. Bridgman, p. 361.

69. Gertrude Stein, *The Geographical History of America; or, The Relation of Human Nature to the Human Mind*, with introductions by Thornton Wilder and William Gass (New York: Vintage Books, 1973), p. 150. (Subsequent references to this work will appear in the text.)

70. Gertrude Stein, "Portraits and Repetition," in *Lectures in America*, p. 181.

71. Gertrude Stein, "Matisse," *Portraits and Prayers* (New York: Random House, 1935), p. 16. Originally published in *Camera Work* (August 1912).

72. Stein, *Picasso*, p. 35.

73. Ibid., p. 13.

74. Ibid., p. 44.

75. Douglas Cooper, *The Cubist Epoch* (New York: Phaidon, 1971), p. 42.

76. Fry, p. 14. See also Fry's discussion of the relationships between Cézanne, cubism, and the ideas of Bergson and Husserl, pp. 38–39.

77. Stein, *Picasso*, pp. 14–15. Stein's discussion of cubism avoids stating that Picasso's work portrays simultaneity, a controversial point. The common discussion of analytic cubist works as "the dissection of analyses of masses, and of the combination of multiple points of view, with implications of a 'fourth dimension' or of non-euclidean geometry," Fry believes to be misunderstanding (p. 24)—and the idea of simultaneity (applied to both literature and art) Fry saw as a rather naïve idea, derived from the writings of Apollinaire, Gleizes, Metzinger, and others, "which has little to do with the essence of cubism" (p. 32). Fry's view is controversial, however. For example, Mitchell, in "Bergson, Le Bon, and Hermetic Cubism," maintains that simultaneity is indeed an important aspect in Picasso and Braque's painting (see p. 179). But the question of the value of Stein's interpretation of cubism aside, it is significant that her explanations of Picasso's work parallel so closely her explanations of what she was doing in writing.

78. Stein, "Portraits and Repetition," p. 179.

79. Ibid., pp. 166–67. For an excellent discussion of Stein's use of repetition, see Bruce F. Kawin, *Telling It Again and Again: Repetition in Literature and Film* (Ithaca: Cornell University Press, 1972), pp. 117–31.

80. Stein, "Portraits and Repetition," pp. 177–78.

81. Stein, *Picasso*, p. 35.

82. The suggestion here is not that in analytic cubism there was always necessarily a model present, but rather that what the cubists were presenting was not so much the subject as the process of perception itself, which years of experience at working from a model had made them familiar with.

83. This similarity is in part due to the common influence of Cézanne. See Steiner, p. 140, for a discussion of Cézanne's ideas about relationships between perception, knowledge, and memory.

84. Steiner, pp. 145–47.

85. I am grateful to Dr. Timothy Mitchell of the department of art history at the University of Kansas for calling my attention to this similarity in texture.

86. Jakobson, *Studies on Child Language and Aphasia*, p. 70. Steiner also believes that the presentation of a person as a list of character traits, as in Stein's early portraits, is "the first step toward synechdoche" (p. 18).

87. Jakobson, *Studies on Child Language and Aphasia*, pp. 57 and 64.

88. I use the term *repetitive* here and elsewhere for the sake of simplicity—but with apologies to Stein. Stein rarely repeats *exactly* what she has written before; there truly is almost always a difference in emphasis.

89. One of the most interesting aspects of Steiner's comparison of Stein's early portraits with analytic cubism is her discussion of geometry and grammar as similar bases of each. Steiner points out that Stein made diagrams (resembling sentence diagrams) of interpersonal relationships (p. 136) and points out that "this linking of a subject and his group to a functional element in a sentence through their common translatability into a grammatical diagram is analogous to the cubists' accommodation of the three-dimensional subject to the picture plane through their common abstract organizational principles—geometry" (p. 139). This analogy is significant, since both diagrams of syntax and geometry reveal relationships based on contiguity. See also p. 147.

90. Gertrude Stein, "Four Dishonest Ones: Told by a Description of What They Do," in *Writings and Lectures*, p. 216.

91. Stein, *Picasso*, p. 15.

92. However, see Marin's analysis of a "reading" of a pictorial image as a sequential process relying to some extent on memory as it is generated through a number of visual circuits through the painting. See Louis Marin, *Études Sémiologiques: Écritures, Peintures* (Paris: Editions Klincksieck, 1971), p. 21.

93. Strother B. Purdy, "Gertrude Stein at Marienbad," *PMLA* 85 (1970):1096.

94. Harold Rosenburg, "The Cubist Epoch," *New Yorker*, May 8, 1971, p. 104.

95. Bridgman, p. 57.

96. This important topic has been discussed by Meyer Shapiro. For example, see his discussion of the possible expressive content of shape and line in his article, "On Some Problems in the Semiotics of Visual Art: Field and Vehicle in Image-Signs," *Semiotica* 1 (1969):230–31, 238.

97. Robert Rosenblum, *Cubism and Twentieth Century Art*, rev. ed. (New York: Harry N. Abrams, 1966), p. 37.

98. Fry, p. 56.

99. Gertrude Stein, "Picasso," in *Portraits and Prayers*, pp. 19–20. Originally published in *Camera Work* (August 1912).

Chapter Two

1. Bridgman, p. 125.

2. Ibid., p. 124.

3. Ibid.

4. Donald Sutherland, *Gertrude Stein: A Biography of Her Work* (New Haven: Yale University Press, 1951), p. 74.

5. Bridgman, p. 124.

6. Stein, "Portraits and Repetition," p. 189.

7. Bridgman, p. 124.

8. Stein, "Portraits and Repetition," pp. 194–95.

9. Leon Katz and Edward Burns, "They Walk in the Light," in *Gertrude Stein on Picasso*, p. 115.

10. Rosenblum, pp. 71–72.

11. Bridgman, p. 124.

12. Weinstein, p. 84.

13. Ibid., p. 62.

14. Ibid., p. 84.

15. This distinction between two kinds of abstraction in Stein's first and second period of obscurity differs significantly from Steiner's distinction between two meanings of abstraction. (See below, ch. 6, p. 110.)

16. Thornton Wilder, introduction to *Four in America*, by Gertrude Stein (New Haven: Yale University Press, 1947), pp. viii–ix.

17. Bridgman, p. 124.

18. Bridgman, in a footnote on p. 125, indicates it is likely that *Tender Buttons* was not composed earlier than 1912.

19. Cooper, p. 188.

20. Ibid.

21. Stein, *Picasso*, pp. 26–28.

22. Stein, "Portraits and Repetition," p. 191.

23. Fry, *Cubism*, pp. 38–39.

24. Steiner, p. 154.

25. Stein, "Portraits and Repetition," pp. 188–89.

26. Stein, *Picasso*, p. 14.

27. Cooper, p. 181. Fry (p. 15) sees the appearance of color as more than decorative but a part of the cubist's attempt to solve the problem of "how to indicate the relation of volumes to each other without the use of chiaroscuro."

28. This appears in color in Cooper, p. 56, plate 45.

29. Stein, *Picasso*, p. 35. Stein's inconsistencies with dates are evident here: on this page she refers to "this last period of pure cubism, 1914–1917" but on p. 37 she dates the same period as 1913–17. In her defense one can say that, in Picasso's work as well as in her own, stylistic changes evolved slowly rather than suddenly.

30. Ibid., p. 37.

31. Ibid., p. 27.

32. Bridgman, p. 103.

33. Gertrude Stein, "Portrait of Mabel Dodge at the Villa Curonia," *Selected Writings of Gertrude Stein*, ed. Carl van Vechten (New York: Random House, 1962), p. 529. It was originally printed privately by Mabel Dodge (1912) and was reprinted in Stein, *Portraits and Prayers* (1943).

34. Bridgman, pp. 361–62. Apparently this work is particularly difficult to date. Bridgman's dating of this work is inconsistent. On p. 120 he dates "The Portrait of Mable Dodge at the Villa Curonia" as 1911 (as does Steiner, p. 89). But *The Autobiography of Alice B. Toklas* corroborates Bridgman's later dating of the visit, placing it after Stein and Toklas's return from Spain (p. 121 in *Selected Writings of Gertrude Stein*), and states that it was during that visit that the portrait was written (p. 123). Brinnin (pp. 152, 170) corroborates the production of that portrait during the visit that followed the 1912 trip to Spain.

35. Cooper, p. 183.

36. Leo Stein, *Journey into the Self*, p. 53.

37. Stein, "Poetry and Grammar," p. 228.

38. Ibid., p. 235.

39. It is interesting that synthetic cubism, though more arbitrary and less "realistic" than analytic cubism, is in some ways "more easily legible" (Fry, p. 30) once one understands the conventions involved. In both synthetic cubism and Stein's second style, specific signifieds are evoked by a more specific concrete vocabulary, and what is left obscure and ambiguous are the relationships (spatial, syntactic) among those signifieds. That people find the result easier to "read" in painting than in writing may be due to differences between the two media. It may also indicate more resistance to learning a new set of verbal conventions than visual conventions.

40. Marjorie Perloff, "Poetry as Word-System: The Art of Gertrude Stein," *American Poetry Review* 8 (September-October, 1979):34.

41. Stein, "Poetry and Grammar," p. 234.

42. Jakobson, *Studies on Child Language and Aphasia*, pp. 63–64.

43. Ibid.

44. Fry maintains that in the early cubist collages, a part of an object would sometimes stand for the whole, so that, for example, in Picasso's *Still Life with Chair Caning*, the first cubist collage, "a section of facsimile caning signifies the whole chair" (p. 27). Assuming that Picasso's intention was to signify a chair (rather than just the caning), it then appears that vestiges of analytic cubism's metonymic orientation appear in the early works of synthetic cubism. But, as Fry points out (pp. 27–28), these pieces of

cut paper soon were used much more arbitrarily, so that in Picasso's *The Violin (Violin and Fruit)* (1913) (Plate 17) newsprint can "signify literally a newspaper on a table," but it can also just as easily signify a bowl.

45. This phenomenon is not limited to *Tender Buttons*, of course. See Perloff, p. 35, for an analysis of how Stein challenges syntax in "Susie Asado" by using verbs and adjectives like nouns and placing auxiliary verbs after, instead of before, main verbs.

46. However, this is *not* to say, as Steiner has suggested (p. 156), that Stein's second style "achieves the same result as the abstract expressionists who did not permit any mimesis in their painting."

47. Stein, "Poetry and Grammar," p. 231.

48. Stein's use of rhythm is an important element in many works of the period. See Perloff, p. 34, for an interesting discussion of Stein's use of rhythm in "Susie Asado."

49. See James's chapter "Association" in *Psychology*, as well as the discussion of the metaphoric and metonymic poles in Jakobson, "Two Aspects of Aphasia," in *Studies on Child Language and Aphasia*.

50. Jakobson, *Studies on Child Language and Aphasia*, p. 67.

51. Fry notes a certain amount of wordplay in the use of newspaper captions in cubist collage (p. 29) as well as a kind of "visual rhyming" repeating key shapes (p. 34). See also Robert Rosenblum's discussion of visual and verbal puns with newspaper captions in "Picasso and the Typography of Cubism," in *Picasso in Retrospect*, ed. Sir Roland Penrose and John Golding (New York: Harper & Row, 1980).

52. Steiner, p. 156.

53. Sutherland, *Gertrude Stein*, p. 77.

54. Stein, "Poetry and Grammar," p. 229.

55. Ibid., p. 232.

Chapter Three

1. Picasso and Gris were the only key figures in the cubist movement who escaped mobilization in 1914 (Fry, p. 32).

2. Bridgman, p. 139.

3. Gertrude Stein, *The Mother of Us All*, in *Last Operas and Plays*, ed. Carl Van Vechten (New York: Rinehart & Co., 1949), p. 55.

4. Weinstein, p. 83.

5. Michel Butor, "The Book as Object," trans. Patricia Dreyfus, in *Inventory: Essays by Michel Butor*, ed. Richard Howard (New York: Simon & Schuster, 1968), p. 44. This essay originally appeared as "Le Livre comme objet" in Butor's *Repertoire II: Études et Conférences 1959–1963* (Paris: Les Éditions de Minuit, 1964).

6. Weinstein, p. 5.

7. Ibid., p. 84.

8. Stein, "Have They Attacked Mary He Giggled," in *Selected Writings of Gertrude Stein*, p. 534. Originally published in *Vanity Fair*, June 1917.

9. Gertrude Stein, "Oval," in *Bee Time Vine and Other Pieces (1913–1927)*, vol. 3 of Unpublished Works of Gertrude Stein, ed. Carl Van Vechten (New York: Books for Libraries Press, 1953), p. 129.

10. Rogers, pp. 113–14.

11. Weinstein, p. 73. This might suggest an analogy with the ready-made collage materials used by Braque and Picasso, especially their use of words cut out of newspapers.

12. Barthes, "Elements of Semiology," p. 19.

13. Jakobson, *Studies on Child Language and Aphasia*, p. 53.

14. Gertrude Stein, "An Exercise in Analysis," in *Last Operas and Plays*, p. 122.

15. Ibid., p. 125.

16. Ibid., p. 129.

17. Ibid., p. 133.

18. Butor, "The Book as Object," pp. 44–45.

19. Gertrude Stein, "What Is English Literature," in *Lectures in America*, pp. 17–18.

20. Gertrude Stein, "Johnny Grey," in *Geography and Plays* (Boston: Four Seas Co., 1922), pp. 168–69.

21. Gertrude Stein, "Plays," in *Lectures in America*, p. 111.

22. Gertrude Stein, *Four Saints in Three Acts*, in *Last Operas and Plays*, p. 462.

23. Bridgman, p. 140. In fact Steiner (p. 95) uses the term *thought conversation* to refer to works of this type.

24. Weinstein, p. 74.

25. Gertrude Stein, *Short Sentences*, in *Last Operas and Plays*, p. 318.

26. Stein, "Plays," p. 109.

27. Gertrude Stein, *Listen to Me*, in *Last Operas and Plays*, p. 415.

28. Stein, *Four Saints in Three Acts*, p. 444.

29. Ibid., p. 461.

30. Gertrude Stein, *They Must. Be Wedded. To Their Wife.*, in *Last Operas and Plays*, pp. 232–33.

31. Stein, *Short Sentences*, p. 319.

32. Gertrude Stein, *Counting Her Dresses*, in *Geography and Plays*, p. 275.

33. Gertrude Stein, *A Play of Pounds*, in *Last Operas and Plays*, p. 247.

34. Gertrude Stein, "Study Nature," in *Bee Time Vine*, p. 182.

35. Gertrude Stein, "All Sunday," in *Alphabets and Birthdays*, Unpublished Works of Gertrude Stein, vol. 7 (New Haven: Yale University Press, 1957), p. 123.

36. Ibid.

37. Jakobson, *Studies on Child Language and Aphasia*, pp. 63–64.

38. Gertrude Stein, "A List," in *Writings and Lectures*, p. 243.

39. Butor, "The Book as Object," p. 46.

40. Gertrude Stein, "IIIIIIIIII," in *Geography and Plays*, p. 189.

41. Stein, "Oval," pp. 140–41.

42. Butor, "The Book as Object," p. 47.

43. Gertrude Stein, "To Do: A Book of Alphabets and Birthdays," in *Alphabets and Birthdays*.

44. Donald Gallup, introduction to *Alphabets and Birthdays*, by Gertrude Stein, p. vii.

45. Stein, "To Do: A Book of Alphabets and Birthdays," p. 3.

46. Butor, "The Book as Object," p. 46.

47. Gertrude Stein, "If I Told Him: A Completed Portrait of Picasso," in *Writings and Lectures*, p. 232.

48. Gertrude Stein, "Composition as Explanation," in *Gertrude Stein: Writings and Lectures*, p. 27.

49. Steiner, pp. 167–68.

50. Stein, "Composition as Explanation," p. 29.

51. Barthes, "Elements of Semiology," p. 58.

52. Stein, "Oval," p. 126.

53. Stein, "A List," p. 255.

54. Ibid., p. 251.

55. Jakobson, *Studies on Child Language and Aphasia*, p. 54.

56. Ibid., p. 41.

57. Stein, "To Do: A Book of Alphabets and Birthdays," p. 81.

58. Butor, "The Book as Object," p. 47.

59. Gertrude Stein, "Birthdays: A Birthday Book," in *Alphabets and Birthdays*, p. 48.

60. Gertrude Stein, "History or Messages from History," ibid., p. 236.

61. William Gass, "Gertrude Stein: Her Escape from Protective Language," *Accent* 18 (Autumn 1958):244.

Chapter Four

1. Steiner (p. 117) notes this tendency toward increased clarity beginning in some of the portraits written between 1926–46. "Some are as difficult as the 1913 portraits, although differently so, while others are as close to straight expository prose as anything in Stein's writing (they are certainly precursors of *The Autobiography of Alice B. Toklas*)." It is interesting that Fry (p. 35) dates the return of "expressive intensity . . . which had so long been suppressed or sublimated" in Picasso's work as beginning in 1925.

2. Steiner, p. 181.

3. Bridgman, p. 363.

4. Ibid., p. 206.

5. Ibid., p. 380.

6. Ibid., p. 206.

7. Ibid., p. 209.

8. Stein, "Study Nature," p. 181.

9. Gertrude Stein, *Ida: A Novel* (New York: Random House, 1941), p. 38. The date of composition supplied by Bridgman (p. 384) is 1940. Subsequent references to this work will appear within the text.

10. Bridgman, p. 205.

11. Brinnin, p. 350.

12. Rogers, p. 114, identifies the source of this phrase as Mother Goose.

13. Brinnin, p. 367.

14. Gertrude Stein, *Everybody's Autobiography* (1937; reprint, New York: Random House, 1973), p. 64.

15. Gertrude Stein, "And Now," *Vanity Fair* 19 (September 1934):65.

16. Gertrude Stein, "Lecture Two," in *Narration* (Chicago: University of Chicago Press, 1935), p. 27.

17. Ibid., p. 28.

18. Copeland, p. 74.

19. Stein, quoted in "A Transatlantic Interview 1946," p. 19.

20. Stein, "Lecture Two," pp. 18–19.

21. Sutherland, *Gertrude Stein*, p. 154.

22. Ibid., pp. 160–66.

23. Ibid., p. 160.

24. It is interesting that *Ida* has also been seen as a female *Bildungsroman*. See, for example, Cynthia Secor, "*Ida*: Great American Novel," *Twentieth Century Literature*

24 (Spring 1979):97, for a discussion of the content of this novel as feminist.

25. Thornton Wilder, introduction to *The Geographical History of America*, p. 47.

26. Ibid., p. 45.

27. Wendell Wilcox, "A Note on Stein and Abstraction," *Poetry* 55 (February 1940):254.

28. Bridgman, p. 261.

29. Stein, "Poetry and Grammar," pp. 229–30.

30. Ibid., p. 231.

31. William H. Gass, introduction to *The Geographical History of America*, p. 23. This introduction is copyrighted 1973.

32. Ibid., p. 33.

33. Wilder, introduction to *The Geographical History of America*, p. 48.

Chapter Five

1. Stein, *Picasso*, p. 30.

2. Ibid., p. 49.

3. Ibid., p. 12.

4. Donald Sutherland, "Gertrude Stein and the Twentieth Century," in *A Primer for the Gradual Understanding of Gertrude Stein*, p. 151.

5. Weinstein, p. 84.

6. Hoffman, p. 197.

7. Weinstein, p. 83.

8. James, *Psychology*, pp. 154–55.

9. Ibid., pp. 356–57.

10. Neil Schmitz, "Gertrude Stein as Post- Modernist: The Rhetoric of *Tender Buttons*," *Journal of Modern Literature* 3 (July 1974):1216.

11. Lane Cooper, *The Rhetoric of Aristotle* (1932; reprint, Appleton-Century-Crofts, 1960), p. 143.

12. Moshe F. Rubinstein, *Patterns of Problem Solving* (Englewood Cliffs, N.J.: Prentice-Hall, 1975), p. 54.

13. Kawin points out that Beckett's repetition is based on "listing the logical permutations in an attempt at problem solving" (p. 134). This seems somewhat similar to Stein's listing of all possibilities.

14. Gertrude Stein, "Mi-Careme," in *Writings and Lectures*, p. 221.

15. Steiner, pp. 67–70.

16. James, *Psychology*, p. 156. See also Steiner's discussion of Stein's ideas and James's theories about identity and thought (pp. 29–31, 42–43).

17. Ibid., p. 243.

18. Steiner sees the a-rose-is-a-rose statement and others like it as examples of "the type of semitautological equation that Stein felt to be especially powerful. It is an 'insistence,' the seeming repetition of a word to catch its referent at each separate moment of its existing" (p. 87).

19. Stein, "Four Dishonest Ones: Told by a Description of What They Do," in *Writings and Lectures*, pp. 218–19.

20. James, *Psychology*, pp. 201–2. Steiner (p. 49) also links Stein's "notion of the personality as a regular succession of 'sames' with constant variations" as similar to James's theories about identity and perception.

21. S. I. Hayakawa, *Language in Thought and Action*, 4th ed. (New York: Harcourt

Brace Jovanovich, 1978), p. 154.

22. See Steiner's discussion of the portrait "Pach" (p. 78), for example, in which Stein "demonstrates the inadequacy of logic in proceeding from empirical evidence in the present to a judgmental prediction of the future," which leads Stein to posit "two identical conclusions dependent on contradictory conditions: 'If he is a young one now he will perhaps be succeeding very well in living. If he is not a young one now he will perhaps be succeeding very well in living.'" Steiner, p. 78, quoting from Gertrude Stein, *Two: Gertrude Stein and Her Brother and Other Early Portraits (1908–1912)*, ed. Carl Van Vechten (New Haven: Yale University Press, 1951), p. 338.

23. Schmitz, "Gertrude Stein as Post-Modernist, pp. 1206–7.

24. Barthes, "Elements of Semiology," p. 50.

25. Perloff, p. 40.

26. Jacqueline Berke, *Twenty Questions for the Writer: A Rhetoric with Readings*, 2d ed. (New York: Harcourt Brace Jovanovich, 1976), p. 35.

27. Perloff points out the irony in Stein's use of the negative definition and says, "Substances are defined by what they are not, but what they *are* remains open to question. And Gertrude Stein wants it that way because her real subject is change" (p. 41).

28. Berke, p. 25.

29. Hayakawa, p. 54. The emphasis is in the original.

30. Rogers (p. 14) identifies this phrase as an "old saw."

Chapter Six

1. Jakobson, *Studies on Child Language and Aphasia*, p. 73.

2. B. F. Skinner, "Has Gertrude Stein a Secret?" *Atlantic Monthly*, January 1934, pp. 50–57.

3. See Skinner, p. 53.

4. Ibid., p. 54.

5. Steiner writes, in response to Skinner's argument, that she doesn't understand why critics "have been so offended at the idea of using techniques from or even the technique of automatic writing. . . . I have tried to show that Stein was an extraordinarily conscious writer. . . . However, anything that Stein observed in her experiments that fit into her scheme was certainly fair game stylistically" (pp. 48–49).

6. Allegra Stewart, *Gertrude Stein and the Present* (Cambridge, Mass.: Harvard University Press, 1967), p. 149.

7. Ibid., p. 88.

8. Ibid., p. 89.

9. Ibid., pp. 91–92.

10. Ibid., p. 91.

11. Ibid., p. 94.

12. Ibid., p. 67.

13. Ibid., pp. 73–74.

14. Brinnin, p. 30.

15. Stewart, p. 72.

16. Ibid.

17. Gertrude Stein, *Things as They Are* (Vermont: Pawlet, 1950).

18. Bridgman, p. 365.

19. Ibid., p. 40.

20. Edmund Wilson, "Gertrude Stein Old and Young," in *Shores of Light: A Literary*

Chronicle of the Twenties and Thirties (New York: Farrar, Straus & Young, 1952), p. 581.

21. Ibid., p. 586.

22. Bridgman, p. xvi.

23. Ibid., pp. 148–50.

24. Ibid., pp. 149–50.

25. Linda Simon, *The Biography of Alice B. Toklas* (New York: Avon Books, 1977–78), pp. 315–17.

26. Elizabeth Fifer, "Is Flesh Advisable? The Interior Theater of Gertrude Stein," *Signs* 4 (Spring 1979):472–83.

27. Ibid., p. 483.

28. Ibid., pp. 477–78.

29. Perloff, p. 41.

30. Fifer, p. 477.

31. Brinnin, p. 127.

32. Sometimes the problem is complicated by comparisons of Stein's writing to surrealism or Dada painting. But looking to Dada to explain the arbitrary nature of Stein's *Tender Buttons* style, as Perloff does (pp. 37, 40), is an unnecessary complication; one need only look to synthetic cubism for this impulse toward the arbitrary. Mellow maintains that although Stein may have influenced the Dadaists, she was never influenced by them. See James R. Mellow, "Gertrude Stein among the Dadaists," *Arts* 51 (May 1977):124.

33. Hoffman, p. 28.

34. In his chapter "Portraits and the Abstract Style," which deals with Stein's early portraits (1908–12), Hoffman states that Stein wanted to use language "plastically," as the cubists did. However, until 1912 the work of Stein and the cubists emphasized *mimesis*, with the "plastic" qualities of the signifying elements taking a back seat until the blossoming of synthetic cubism (or the *Tender Buttons* style). Hoffman's reference to the fragmentation of forms by Braque and Picasso, a phenomenon related to analytic cubism, confuses the issues somewhat; and his reference to what "the painters of the period" were doing—by examining Picasso's *Girl before A Mirror*—does not clarify what was happening in 1908–12, since that work was painted in 1932. See Hoffman, p. 170.

35. Steiner, p. 133.

36. Oscar Cargill, *Intellectual America: Ideas on the March* (New York: Macmillan Co., 1941), p. 319.

37. Ibid., p. 320.

38. Gertrude Stein, "Susie Asado," quoted by Cargill, p. 320. This passage appears in *Geography and Plays*, p. 13.

39. Cargill, pp. 321–22.

40. Ibid., p. 321.

41. Brinnin, p. 134.

42. Ibid., p. 142.

43. Ibid., pp. 143–44.

44. Steiner, p. 160.

45. Ibid., pp. 12–13.

46. Wilcox, "A Note on Stein and Abstractionism," p. 257.

47. Sutherland, *Gertrude Stein*, p. 200.

48. Stewart, pp. 34–35.

49. Harry Garvin, "Sound and Sense in *Four Saints in Three Acts*," *Bucknell Review* 5 (December 1954):5.

50. Ibid., p. 3. See also pp. 4–5 for Garvin's metaphysical gloss of a passage from act 2, scene 2, of the same work.

51. Sutherland, *Gertrude Stein*, p. 77.

52. Harry Garvin, "How to *Read* Gertrude Stein" (paper presented before the Modern Language Association Convention at New York in 1974), p. 5.

53. Ibid., p. 6.

54. Steiner, pp. 97–98.

55. Ibid.

56. Sutherland, "Gertrude Stein and the Twentieth Century," p. 152.

57. Weinstein, p. 56.

58. Hoffman, p. 18.

59. Brinnin, p. 304.

60. Gertrude Stein, *The Autobiography of Alice B. Toklas*, in *Selected Writings of Gertrude Stein*, p. 72. Originally published New York: Harcourt, Brace & Co., 1933.

61. Purdy, p. 1096.

62. Garvin, "How to *Read* Gertrude Stein," pp. 4–5.

63. Purdy, p. 1102.

64. One major exception to this neglect of Stein is Bruce Kawin's *Telling It Again and Again*, which places Stein's work in the context of other literature and film using repetition, and relates Stein to a group of significant writers ranging from Proust to Beckett, Resnais, and Robbe-Grillet.

65. Carolyn Faunce Copeland, *Language and Time and Gertrude Stein* (Iowa City: University of Iowa Press, 1975), p. 1.

66. Schmitz, "Gertrude Stein as Post- Modernist," p. 1203.

67. Stein, "Composition as Explanation," in *Writings and Lectures*, p. 23.

68. Nathalie Sarraute, *The Age of Suspicion*, trans. Maria Jolas (New York: Braziller, 1963), pp. 53–54. Originally published as *L'Ere de soupçon* (Paris: Éditions Gallimard, 1956).

69. Alain Robbe-Grillet, *For a New Novel: Essays on Fiction*, trans. Richard Howard (New York: Grove Press, 1963), p. 28. Originally published as *Pour un nouveau roman* (Paris: Les Éditions de Minuit, 1963).

70. Stein, quoted in "A Transatlantic Interview 1946," pp. 21–22.

71. Bridgman, p. 366.

72. See Ethel F. Cornwall's "Gertrude Stein: Forerunner of Nathalie Sarraute," *International Fiction Review* 5 (July 1978):91–95, for a discussion of ways in which Stein's work anticipates that of Nathalie Sarraute, particularly by virtue of the theoretical and psychological approach of both writers, their similar interest in language at the preverbal level (or "sub-conversations") and the resulting abstract style of each.

73. Michel Butor, *Niagara*, trans. Elinor S. Miller (Chicago: Henry Regnery Company, 1969), p. 48. Originally published as *6 810 000 Litres d'eau par seconde: Étude stéréophonique* (Paris: Éditions Gallimard, 1965).

74. Stein, "Portraits and Repetition," p. 184.

75. Robbe-Grillet, *For a New Novel*, p. 33.

76. Stein, "What Are Masterpieces and Why Are There So Few of Them," *Writings and Lectures*, p. 150. Originally published in *What Are Masterpieces* (Los Angeles: Conference Press, 1940).

77. Sarraute, pp. 84–85.

78. For an extended comparison between Stein's work and Beckett's on the basis of repetition and use of present tense in the theater, see Kawin, pp. 128–53. Kawin, in comparing *Waiting for Godot* with *Four Saints in Three Acts*, says that both are "plays of landscape" (p. 149).

79. Kawin, p. 146.

80. Michael Butor, "Research on the Technique of the Novel," in *Inventory: Essays by Michel Butor*, trans. and ed. Richard Howard (New York: Simon & Schuster, 1968), p. 19. This essay was originally published as "Recherches sur la technique du roman" (Paris: Les Éditions de Minuit, 1964).

81. Ibid.

82. Robbe-Grillet, introduction to *Last Year at Marienbad*, trans. Richard Howard (New York: Grove Press, 1962), p. 13. Published as *L'Année dernière a Marienbad* (Paris: Les Éditions de Minuit, 1961).

83. Garvin, "How to *Read* Gertrude Stein," p. 4.

Appendix

1. In the text Bridgman disagrees with the Yale Catalogue's date; he says *Tender Buttons* could not have been written earlier than 1912. See *Gertrude Stein in Pieces*, footnote on p. 125.

2. The *Yale Catalogue* dates this as 1911, but other evidence from *The Autobiography of Alice B. Toklas* places this work after Stein's return from Spain in 1912. Bridgman corroborates the 1912 date for the visit to Mabel Dodge's Villa, p. 363, as does Brinnin. For further discussion, see footnote 34 for chapter 2 above.

Primary Sources

Stein, Gertrude. "And Now." *Vanity Fair* 19 (September 1934):35.
———. *Alphabets and Birthdays*. The Unpublished Works of Gertrude Stein, vol. 7. Edited by Carl Van Vechten. New Haven: Yale University Press, 1951.
———. *The Autobiography of Alice B. Toklas*. New York: Harcourt, Brace & Co., 1933.
———. *Bee Time Vine and Other Pieces (1913–1917)*. The Unpublished Writings of Gertrude Stein, vol. 3. Edited by Carl Van Vechten. New York: Arno Press, Books for Libraries, 1953.
———. *Everybody's Autobiography*. New York: Random House, 1937.
———. *The Geographical History of America, or The Relation of Human Nature to the Human Mind*. New York: Vintage Books, 1973.
———. *Geography and Plays*. Boston: Four Seas Company, 1922.
———. *Ida: A Novel*. New York: Random House, 1941.
———. *Lectures in America*. Boston: Beacon Press, 1935.
———. *Last Operas and Plays*. Edited by Carl Van Vechten. New York: Rinehart & Co., 1949.
———. *The Making of Americans: Being a History of a Family's Progress*. Complete Version. New York: Something Else Press, 1966.
———. *Narration*. Chicago: University of Chicago Press, 1935.

————. *Picasso*. Boston: Beacon Press, 1959.

————. *Portraits and Prayers*. New York: Random House, 1935.

————. *Selected Writings of Gertrude Stein*. Edited by Carl Van Vechten. New York: Random House, 1962.

————. "A Transatlantic Interview 1946." In *A Primer for the Gradual Understanding of Gertrude Stein*, edited by Robert Bartlett Haas. Los Angeles: Black Sparrow Press, 1971.

————. *Tender Buttons*. New York: Claire-Marie, 1914.

————. *Things as They Are*. Vermont: Pawlet, 1950.

————. *What Are Masterpieces*. New York: Pitman Publishing Corp., 1940.

————. *Writings and Lectures 1909–1945*. Edited by Patricia Meyerowitz. Baltimore: Penguin Books, 1971.

Secondary Sources

Arnason, H. A. *The History of Modern Art: Painting, Sculpture, Architecture*. Englewood Cliffs, N.J.: Prentice- Hall, n.d.

Ashton, Dore. *Picasso on Art: A Selection of Views*. New York: Viking Press, 1972.

Bassoff, Bruce. "Gertrude Stein's 'Composition as Explanation.'" *Twentieth Century Literature* 24 (Spring 1978):76–80.

Barrett, William. *Irrational Man: A Study in Existential Philosophy*. New York: Doubleday & Co., 1958.

Barthes, Roland. *Writing Degree Zero and Elements of Semiology*. Translated by Annette Lavers and Colin Smith. Boston: Beacon Press, 1974. Originally published as *Le Degré zéro de l'écriture suivi de Éléments de sémiologie*. Paris: Éditions du Seuil, 1953.

Berke, Jacqueline. *Twenty Questions for the Writer: A Rhetoric with Readings*. 2d ed. New York: Harcourt Brace Jovanovich, 1976.

Bridgman, Richard. *Gertrude Stein in Pieces*. New York: Oxford University Press, 1970.

Brinnin, John Malcolm. *The Third Rose: Gertrude Stein and Her World*. Boston: Little, Brown & Co., 1959.

Burns, Edward. "Gertrude Stein: Selected Criticism," *Twentieth Century Literature* 24 (Summer 1978):127–34.

Burnham, Jack. *The Structure of Art*. Rev. ed. New York: Braziller, 1971.

Butor, Michel. *Niagara*. Translated by Elinor S. Miller. Chicago: Henry Regnery Co., 1969. Originally published as *6 810 000 litres d'eau par seconde: Étude stéréophonique*. Paris: Éditions Gallimard, 1965.

————. "The Novel as Research" and "The Book as Object." Translated by Patricia Dreyfus. In *Inventory: Essays by Michel Butor*, edited by Richard Howard. New York: Simon & Schuster, 1968. These essays originally appeared as *Répertoire II: Etudes et conférences 1959–1963*. Paris: Les Éditions de Minuit, 1964.

Cargill, Oscar. *Intellectual America: Ideas on the March*. New York: Macmillan Co., 1941.

Cooper, Douglas. *The Cubist Epoch*. New York: Phaidon, 1971.

Cooper, Lane. *The Rhetoric of Aristotle*. 1932. Reprint. New York: Appleton-Century-Crofts, 1960.

Cornwall, Elizabeth F. "Gertrude Stein: Forerunner of Nathalie Sarraute." *International Fiction Review* 5 (July 1978):91–95.

Copeland, Carolyn Faunce. *Language and Time and Gertrude Stein*. Iowa City: University of Iowa Press, 1975.

Corke, Hilary. "Reflections on a Great Stone Face: The Achievement of Gertrude Stein." *Kenyon Review* 23 (Summer 1961):367–89.

Cullers, Jonathan. *Structuralist Poetics: Structuralism, Linguistics and the Study of Literature*. Ithaca: Cornell University Press, 1975.

Daix, Pierre, and Rosselet, Joan, comps. *Picasso: The Cubist Years 1907–1916: A Catalogue Raisonné of the Paintings and Related Works*. New York: New York Graphic Society/Little, Brown & Co., 1979.

Dorfman, G. and G. "Reaffirming Painting: A Critique of Structuralist Criticism." *Art Forum* 16 (October 1977):59–65.

Dubnick, Randa. "Metaphor and Metonymy in the Paintings of René Magritte," *Contemporary Literature* 21 (Summer 1980):407–19.

———. "Two Types of Obscurity in the Writings of Gertrude Stein." *Emporia State Research Studies* 24 (Winter 1976):5–27.

Fifer, Elizabeth. "Is Flesh Advisable? The Interior Theater of Gertrude Stein." *Signs* 4 (Spring 1979):472–83.

"Flat Prose." *Atlantic Monthly* 114 (September 1914):430–32.

Fry, Edward. *Cubism*. London: Thames & Hudson, 1966. Reprint. New York: Oxford University Press, 1978.

Gallup, Donald. "Introduction." *Alphabets and Birthdays*, by Gertrude Stein. The Unpublished Writings of Gertrude Stein, vol. 7. Edited by Carl Van Vechten. New Haven: Yale University Press, 1951.

Garvin, Harry. "How to *Read* Gertrude Stein". Paper read at Modern Language Association Convention, 1974, at New York. Mimeographed.

———. "Sound and Sense in *Four Saints in Three Acts*." *Bucknell Review* 5 (December 1954):1–11.

Gass, William H. "Gertrude Stein: Her Escape from Protective Language." *Accent* 18 (Autumn 1958): 233–44.

———. Introduction to *The Geographical History of America; or, The Relation of Human Nature to the Human Mind*, by Gertrude Stein. New York: Vintage Books, 1973.

Golding, John. *Cubism: A History and an Analysis, 1907–1914*. 2d ed. London: Faber & Faber, 1968.

De George, Richard and Fernande, eds. *The Structuralists: From Marx to Levi-Strauss*. New York: Doubleday, 1972.

Haas, Robert Bartlett. "Another Garland for Gertrude Stein." In *What Are Masterpieces*, by Gertrude Stein. New York: Pitman Publishing Corporation, 1940.

Hawkes, Terrence. *Structuralism and Semiotics*. Berkeley: University of California Press, 1977.

Hayakawa, S. I. *Language in Thought and Action*. 4th ed. New York: Harcourt Brace Jovanovich, 1978.

Hobhouse, Janet. *Everybody Who Was Anybody: A Biography of Gertrude Stein*. New York: G. P. Putnam's Sons, n.d.

Hoffman, Michael J. *The Development of Abstractionism in the Writings of Gertrude Stein*. Philadelphia: University of Pennsylvania Press, 1965.

―――. *Gertrude Stein*. Boston: Twayne, 1976.

Jakobson, Roman. *Studies on Child Language and Aphasia*. Janua Linguarum, Series Minor, no. 114. The Hague: Mouton & Co., 1971.

―――. "Two Aspects of Language and Two Types of Aphasic Disturbances." In *Fundamentals of Language*, by Roman Jakobson and Morris Halle. Janua Linguarum, no. 50. The Hague: Mouton & Co., 1956.

James, William. *Psychology: Briefer Course*. New York: Henry Holt & Co., 1892.

Katz, Leon. "The First Making of *The Making of Americans*: A Study Based on Her Notebooks and Early Versions of Her Novel (1902–1908)." Ph.D. dissertation, Columbia University, 1963.

―――, and Burns, Edward. "They Walk in the Light." In *Gertrude Stein on Picasso*. Edited by Edward Burns. New York: Liveright Publishing Corp., 1970.

Kawin, Bruce F. *Telling It Again and Again: Repetition in Literature and Film*. Ithaca: Cornell University Press, 1972.

Kibbey, Ray Anne. *Picasso: A Comprehensive Bibliography*. New York: Garland, 1977.

Kristeva, Julia. *Desire in Language: A Semiotic Approach to Literature and Art*. Translated by Thomas Gora, Alice Jardine, and Leon S. Roudiez. Edited by Leon S. Roudiez. New York: Columbia University Press, 1980.

Levi-Strauss, Claude. "The Structural Study of Myth." *Structural Anthropology*. Translated by Claire Jacobson and Brooke Grundfest Scheopf. New York: Harper & Row, Basic Books, 1963. Originally published as *Anthropologie Structurale*. Paris: Plon, 1958.

Levinson, Ronald. "Gertrude Stein, William James, and Grammar." *American Journal of Psychology* 54 (January 1941): 124–28.

Lewis, Wyndam. *Time and Western Man*. New York: Harcourt Brace & Co., 1928.

Liston, Maureen R. *Gertrude Stein: An Annotated Critical Bibliography*. Kent: Kent State University Press, 1979.

Lodge, David. "Gertrude Stein." In *The Modes of Modernist Fiction: Metaphor, Metonymy and the Typology of Modern Literature*. London: Edward Arnold, 1977.

―――. "The Language of Modernist Fiction." *Modernism: 1890–1930*. Edited by Malcolm Bradbury and James MacFarlane. Atlantic Highlands, N.J.: Humanities Press, 1978.

McMillan, Samuel. "Gertrude Stein, the Cubists, and the Futurists." Ph.D. dissertation, University of Texas, 1964.

Marin, Louis. *Études Sémiologiques: Écritures, Peintures*. Paris: Éditions Klinksieck, 1971.

Mellow, James R. *Charmed Circle: Gertrude Stein and Company*. New York: Avon Books, 1974.

―――. "Gertrude Stein among the Dadaists." *Arts* 51 (May 1977):124–26.

Mitchell, Timothy. "Bergson, Le Bon, and Hermetic Cubism." *Journal of Aesthetics and Art Criticism* 36 (Winter 1977):175–83.

Moore, Marianne. "The Spare American Emotion." *Dial* 80 (February 1926):153–56.

Perloff, Marjorie. "Poetry as Word System: The Art of Gertrude Stein." *American Poetry Review* 8 (September-October 1979):33–42.

Porter, Katharine. "Everybody Is a Real One," "Second Wind," and "The Wooden Umbrella." In *The Days Before*. New York: Harcourt Brace, 1952.

Purdy, Strother P. "Gertrude Stein at Marienbad." *PMLA* 85 (1970):1096–1105.

Reid, B. L. *Art by Subtraction: A Dissenting Opinion of Gertrude Stein*. Norman: University of Oklahoma Press, 1958.

Richardson, John. "Your Show of Shows." *New York Review of Books*, July 17, 1980, pp. 16–17.

Robbe-Grillet, Alain. *Last Year at Marienbad*. Translated by Richard Howard. New York: Grove Press, 1962. First published as *L'Année dernière à Marienbad*. Paris: Les Éditions de Minuit, 1961.

―――. *For a New Novel: Essays on Fiction*. Translated by Richard Howard. New York: Grove Press, 1963. First published as *Pour un nouveau roman*. Paris: Editions Gallimard, 1964.

Rogers, W. G. *When This You See Remember Me: Gertrude Stein in Person*. New York: Avon Books, 1948.

Ronnebeck, Arnold. "Gertrude Was Always Giggling." *Books Abroad* 19 (Winter 1945):3–7.

Rosenberg, Harold. "The Cubist Epoch." *New Yorker*, May 8, 1971, pp. 102–5.

Rosenblum, Robert. *Cubism and Twentieth Century Art*. Rev. ed. New York: Harry N. Abrams, 1966.

————. "Picasso and the Typography of Cubism." In *Picasso in Retrospect*, edited by Sir Roland Penrose and John Golding. New York: Harper & Row, 1980.

Rubin, William, ed. *Pablo Picasso: A Retrospective*. Chronology by Jane Fluegel. New York: Museum of Modern Art/New York Graphic Society, 1980.

Rubenstein, Moshe F. *Patterns of Problem Solving*. Englewood Cliffs, N.J.: Prentice-Hall, 1975.

Russell, Frances. *Three Studies in Twentieth Century Obscurity*. Chester Springs, Pa.: Dufour Editions, 1959.

Sarraute, Nathalie. *The Age of Suspicion*. Translated by Maria Jolas. New York: Braziller, 1963. Originally published as *L'Ere du soupçon*. Paris: Éditions Gallimard, 1956.

de Saussure, Ferdinand. *Course in General Linguistics*. Translated by Wade Baskin. New York: McGraw-Hill, 1966. Originally published as *Cours de linguistique général*, edited by Charles Bally, Albert Sechehaye and Albert Reidlinger. Paris: Payot, 1915.

Secor, Cynthia. "Ida, Great American Novel." *Twentieth Century Literature* 24 (Spring 1978): 96–107.

Schmitz, Neil. "Gertrude Stein as Post-Modernist: The Rhetoric of *Tender Buttons*." *Journal of Modern Literature* 3 (July 1975):1203–18.

————. "Portrait, Patriarch and Mythos: The Revenge of Gertrude Stein." *Salmagundi* 40 (Winter 1978):69–91.

Scholes, Robert. *Structuralism in Literature: An Introduction*. New Haven: Yale University Press, 1974.

Shapiro, Meyer. "On Some Problems in the Semiotics of Visual Art: Field and Vehicle in Image-Signs." *Semiotica* 1 (1969):223–42.

Simon, Linda. *The Biography of Alice B. Toklas*. Garden City, N.Y.: Doubleday & Co., 1977.

Skinner, B. F. "Has Gertrude Stein a Secret?" *Atlantic Monthly*, January 1934, pp. 50–57.

Sprigge, Elizabeth. *Gertrude Stein: Her Life and Work*. New York: Harper Brothers, 1951.

Stein, Leo. *Journey into the Self: Being the Letters, Papers and Journals of Leo Stein*. Edited by Edmund Fuller. New York: Crown Publishers, 1950.

Steiner, Wendy. *Exact Resemblance to Exact Resemblance: The Literary Portraiture of Gertrude Stein*. New Haven: Yale University Press, 1980.

Stewart, Allegra. *Gertrude Stein and the Present*. Cambridge: Harvard University Press, 1951.

Sutherland, Donald. *Gertrude Stein: A Biography of Her Work*. New Haven: Yale University Press, 1951.

————. "Gertrude Stein and the Twentieth Century." In *A Primer for the Gradual Understanding of Gertrude Stein*, edited by Robert Bartlett Haas. Los Angeles: Black Sparrow Press, 1971.

Wallis, Mieczytaw. *Arts and Signs*. Studies in Semiotics, 2. Bloomington: Indiana University Press, 1975.

Weinstein, Norman. *Gertrude Stein and the Literature of the Modern Consciousness*. New York: Frederick Ungar, 1970.

Wilcox, Wendell. "A Note on Stein and Abstractionism." *Poetry* 55 (February 1940):254–57.

Wilder, Thornton. Introduction to *Four in America*, by Gertrude Stein. New Haven: Yale University Press, 1947.

————. Introduction to *The Geographical History of America, or The Relation of Human Nature to the Human Mind*, by Gertrude Stein. New York: Vintage Books, 1973.

Williams, William Carlos. "The Work of Gertrude Stein." *Pagany* 1 (Winter 1930):41–46.

Wilson, Edmund. *Axel's Castle: A Study in the Imaginative Literature of 1870–1930*. New York: Charles Scribner's Sons, 1931.

————. "Gertrude Stein Old and Young." In *Shores of Light: A Literary Chronicle of the Twenties and Thirties*. New York: Farrar, Straus, & Young, 1952.

Wittig, Susan. *Structuralism: An Interdisciplinary Study*. Pittsburg: Pickwick Press, 1975.

Yalden-Thomson, D. C. "Obscurity, Exhibition, and Gertrude Stein." *Virginia Quarterly Review* 34 (Winter 1958):133–37.

RANDA DUBNICK WAS BORN in Pueblo, Colorado. She received her B.A. (1970), M.A. (1973), and Ph.D. (1976) from the University of Colorado at Boulder. She is currently on the English faculty at the University of Kansas at Lawrence.